RED COATS
&
GREY JACKETS

RED COATS
&
GREY JACKETS

THE BATTLE *of* CHIPPAWA
5 July 1814

DONALD E. GRAVES

Dundurn Press
Toronto & Oxford

THE ONTARIO HISTORICAL SOCIETY

Toronto; Jim Kochan of Morristown, NJ; Mikhail Murgoci of Toronto; and the editors of *Canadian Geographic Magazine* and *Canadian Military History* journal.

A vote of thanks must go to S. James Gooding, editor of *Arms Collecting*, for permission to use material contained in my article on the artillery of the War of 1812 that appeared in Volume 30, No. 2 (1992) of that periodical.

A very special mention is due to a partner in my work whom I have overlooked in the past. Yet again, Bill Constable, Canada's foremost military cartographer, has managed to translate my chicken scratches into intelligible and beautifully drawn maps.

Finally, for permission to publish the research I conducted for the Department of National Defence, I would like to thank Dr. W.A.B. Douglas, director-general, Directorate of History, and Dr. Steve Harris, then senior historian.

CHAPTER 1

WAR COMES TO THE NIAGARA

On the 25th of June 1812, a small boat put out into the Niagara River from the dock below Fort George, Upper Canada. In the stern, resplendent in scarlet uniform with green facings and gold lace, sat John Baskerville Glegg, captain in His Britannic Majesty's 49th Regiment of Foot and aide-de-camp to Major General Isaac Brock, the British commander in Upper Canada. Glegg was on an official mission to Captain Nathaniel Leonard, commanding officer of Fort Niagara, the American post opposite. He knew Leonard personally – the officers of both forts were frequent visitors to each other's messes and they, and their families, often attended church together in the village of Newark (modern Niagara-on-the-Lake), located directly across the river from Fort Niagara.

This day, Glegg had a more serious purpose. He was to inquire whether Leonard had received official word from his government of the recent declaration of war by the United States against Great Britain. News of this event had reached Brock and, in the courteous fashion of the times, he wanted to confirm it with his opposite number before commencing hostilities.

As the boat reached the mid-point of the river, it picked up the swift current that parallels the American shore, and the rowers rested while the helmsman guided the craft to the dock of the American post. Glegg's business did not take long as Leonard quickly informed him that he had received no official word from Washington. Before leaving, the two officers may have reminisced about happier times and probably wished each other luck as, the next time they met, it would be as enemies. War had come to the Niagara.[1]

Conflict was no stranger to the region. Control of the Niagara peninsula, a major route from the basin of the St. Lawrence to the rich fur-trading area of the upper lakes, was crucial for westward communication. The French had early recognized the peninsula's strategic importance by erecting a fort at the river's mouth in 1727. This Fort Niagara fell to a British siege in 1759 and Britain then retained it for the next thirty-six years. When it was evacuated in 1796, under the terms of the Jay Treaty, Britain maintained her military presence in the area by erecting two new posts: Fort George at the northern end of the river and Fort Erie at the southern.

The last decades of the eighteenth century brought a flurry of settlers to the Niagara. They were attracted to the peninsula not only because of its convenient geographic situation but also by its agricultural promise. The Niagara possessed impressive forests and this bounty was matched by a rich soil particularly suited for orchards. The newcomers set to work industriously and both sides of the river soon reached a fairly advanced state of settlement. By the summer of 1812, the Niagara was a happy and prosperous region far removed from the distant tensions that had led to war between the United States and Great Britain.

Most simply put, the origins of this conflict can be reduced to two main causes – the westward expansion of the American frontier, and the economic consequences of the great war in Europe waged since 1793. By the terms of the treaty that ended the Revolutionary War, the aboriginal nations of the northwest (modern day Michigan, Ohio, Indiana, and Illinois), which had fought on Britain's side, now came within the territorial boundaries of the infant United States. These nations had formed a confederacy to resist the encroaching tide of white settlement but were defeated by superior American military forces in 1794. Many Americans suspected that Britain instigated and supported the resistance of these northwest nations, and these suspicions were enhanced in 1811 when another native confederacy, led by the charismatic Shawnee warrior, Tecumseh, was defeated and its survivors fled to Canada. As a result, not a few Americans in the western states and territories began to agitate for war against Great Britain as the only way to prevent a reoccurrence of troubles on the frontier.

Another source of tension arose out of the general war in Europe against revolutionary and imperial France. After superior British seapower had cleared the French merchant marine from the seas, American shipowners stepped into the vacuum and reaped profits trading with both belligerents. But when Britain and France passed a series of decrees forbidding neutral ships that traded with one, to trade with the other, these same shipowners were caught in the middle. Worse was the high-handed attitude of the Royal Navy, which entered American territorial waters with impunity and impressed American seamen at will. In 1807, war almost broke out when a British warship, HMS *Leopard,* fired on an American warship, USS *Chesapeake,* that refused to give up members of her crew which the British captain claimed were deserters from the Royal Navy.

To force Britain and France to recognize American maritime rights,

President Thomas Jefferson resorted to economic retaliation. Between 1806 and 1810, the U.S. Congress passed legislation curtailing American trade with either belligerent. Unfortunately these measures proved more harmful to American commerce than to the two European enemies and caused much resentment in the coastal and border states whose economies were dependent on foreign trade. When Britain did not respond to this tactic, a "war hawk" faction within the governing Republican party began to press for a military solution to America's grievances. In the autumn and winter of 1811 the young republic became increasingly strident, and by the following spring, war was certain.

The American declaration of hostilities on 18 June 1812 came as no surprise to Lieutenant General Sir George Prevost, the commander-in-chief of British North America. Prevost had only 8400 troops to defend the Canadas and placed most of them around Montreal. If things got bad, he was ready to withdraw from Upper Canada, concentrate at Montreal, and hold on until help arrived from Britain. Confident that the war would shortly be brought to a diplomatic end, he resolved not to attack American territory but to adopt a defensive strategy of "wary measures and occasional daring enterprises" that suited his essentially cautious nature.[2]

This strategy did not please Major General Brock, Prevost's subordinate in Upper Canada. To defend a province whose borders and line of communication along the St. Lawrence were open to attack, Brock had only twelve hundred regular troops and about ten thousand militia. He did possess two advantages – one was the Provincial Marine, a small local navy whose ships controlled Lakes Ontario and Erie; the other was the psychological impact of Britain's native allies that he hoped would offset superior American numbers. The aggressive Brock wanted to take the offensive but was restrained by Prevost who felt British "numbers would not justify offensive operations … unless they were solely calculated to strengthen a defensive attitude."[3]

Upper Canada faced internal as well as external enemies. In the previous two decades thousands of Americans had settled in the province, and they now outnumbered the original Loyalist population. One commentator put their number at more than half Upper Canada's seventy-seven thousand inhabitants. Brock worried about the allegiance of these people, and his suspicions were confirmed in February 1812 when the Legislative Assembly of Upper Canada refused to pass measures he thought essential to strengthen the province for war. Angered, Brock complained to his superior about the "great influence which the numerous settlers from the United States" possessed over the assembly.[4]

American leaders were confident that the conquest of Canada could be achieved with little time and trouble. They miscalculated. The United

States was not prepared for an offensive war – her peacetime army was small and scattered in small garrisons, while recruiting for a larger wartime force, both regular and militia, went slowly. There was a lack of all military *materiel*, and the only experienced military leaders available were aging veterans of the Revolutionary War. Nonetheless, President James Madison's cabinet drew up a somewhat grandiose plan that directed major offensives against Montreal and the western part of Upper Canada with subsidiary operations against Kingston and the Niagara.

The first of these offensives got off to a shaky start in July 1812 when an army under Brigadier General William Hull made a quick stab across the Detroit River into Canada before withdrawing to American territory. News of this incursion reached Brock at York (present-day Toronto) where he was trying to convince the recalcitrant Legislative Assembly to pass defence measures. Using the vessels of the Provincial Marine, Brock moved west with every available regular and militiaman and proceeded to lay siege to Hull's superior force at Detroit. Then, in an act of bravado, Brock demanded that Hull surrender and, more amazing still, Hull did exactly that.

The victory at Detroit convinced many of the doubtful in Upper Canada that the province would now remain a British possession. The militia, many of whom had been reluctant to turn out when called, now came forth in larger numbers. Some of the more pro-American element in the population departed for the United States while others became vocal in their support for the British Crown. There was cause for hope for it appeared the war would soon be over as, on instructions from London, Prevost had arranged for a suspension of hostilities along the northern frontier. But hopes for an early end to the war were dashed on 4 September 1812 when Madison rejected British peace proposals.

Upper Canada now faced a renewed threat of attack and this time the target was the Niagara peninsula. In the early morning of 13 October, a mixed force of U.S. regulars and militia under New York (Militia) Colonel Solomon Van Rensselaer crossed the Niagara River and seized Queenston Heights. Brock was killed leading a counterattack. Van Rennselaer was wounded and practical command of the American force devolved upon Lieutenant Colonel Winfield Scott, an aggressive twenty-six-year-old regular officer. Scott was unable to prevent Brock's successor from flanking his position and forcing him back to the river. He surrendered after some brisk fighting and the second American invasion of Upper Canada came to an end.

The last two invasion attempts in 1812 fared just as poorly. Following the battle of Queenston Heights, a local armistice went into effect along the

Niagara River until it was cancelled in late November by the new American commander, Brigadier General Alexander Smyth, who was determined to invade Canada before the onset of winter. On 28 November, an American advance party crossed the Niagara a few miles below Fort Erie but was defeated before its main body could reinforce it. Further east, a movement against Montreal by Major General Henry Dearborn was halted when most of his militia refused to cross the international border. Cold weather then terminated active campaigning.

In the spring of 1813, the United States again went on the offensive. Having learned its lesson, the American government constructed naval squadrons on Lakes Ontario and Erie as the necessary first step and, by April, the Lake Ontario naval force was strong enough for offensive operations. Although Secretary of War John Armstrong identified Kingston as the most important objective, he was dissuaded from attacking it by Dearborn and Commodore Isaac Chauncey, the American naval commander, who, instead, proposed an attack on York, followed by an offensive in the Niagara region. On 27 April 1813, Dearborn's troops captured York after a brief battle and occupied it for a few days before sailing for Fort Niagara.

The British commander in the Niagara region, Brigadier General John Vincent, had assembled about one thousand regulars but could only count on the services of about three hundred militia, well below the numbers he needed. The capture of York had soured the mood of euphoria induced by the victories of the previous year, and many Canadians were again convinced of the inevitability of American success. Vincent complained of the militia's "indifference to the important cause to which we are now engaged in."[5] Some elements of the local population had gone further and were actively aiding the Americans – Vincent had received a petition from loyal citizens asking him to declare martial law because of "traitors joining, the Enemy, and some fostered among ourselves."[6]

As the mist rose from Lake Ontario at dawn on 27 May 1813, a line of American boats headed for the Canadian shore west of the Niagara river mouth. Commanded by Winfield Scott, the lead American brigade landed in good order and engaged in a hotly contested battle with Vincent's regulars. The British suffered from the guns of U.S. warships covering the landing and withdrew to Fort George. When the following American brigades landed, the landing force formed in line and then, with fifes and drums playing "Yankee Doodle," advanced through the village of Newark toward the fort. Vincent retreated in good order towards Burlington Bay (modern Hamilton) at the head of the lake. The next day another American force crossed the Niagara and occupied Fort Erie, bringing the entire Canadian side of the river under American control.[7]

The capture of Fort George, however, proved the high point of Dearborn's campaign. When an advance toward Burlington Bay was stopped after a vicious night action at Stoney Creek on 6 June, and another American force was captured at Beaver Dams on 24 June 1813, Dearborn gave up the initiative and, suffering from illness, turned over command to Brigadier General John Boyd. Boyd, under orders from Armstrong to "pay the utmost attention to the instruction & discipline of [his] Troops and engage in no affair with the Enemy" unless absolutely unavoidable, obeyed these instructions to the letter and kept his army in the immediate vicinity of Fort George throughout the summer.[8] Here they wasted away from sickness while contained loosely by a numerically inferior British force. As one observer commented, the U.S. army at Fort George was "panic-struck – shut up, and whipped in by a few hundred miserable Savages."[9]

The presence of American troops on Canadian soil acted as a magnet for those Upper Canadians who sympathized with the United States. In early June, Joseph Willcocks, newspaper editor and member of the Legislative Assembly, appeared in the American lines with an offer to raise a "Corps of Volunteers to assist in changing the Government of this Province into a Republic."[10] His offer was accepted and, in a short time, Willcocks, now a major of United States Volunteers, was leading a unit of mounted scouts that guided American patrols and took the opportunity to settle personal scores with their former countrymen. Caught between two armies and suffering from the depredations of Willcocks and various units of American "volunteers" who crossed the Niagara River to "assist" Boyd's regulars, many locals abandoned their homes and fled to the safety of the British lines.

In late August, Boyd was superseded by Major General James Wilkinson. Under Armstrong's orders, Wilkinson transferred most of the American regulars from the Niagara area to Sackets Harbor for another attempt at Kingston. But again, Armstrong let himself be talked out of attacking it in favour of a risky scheme to move Wilkinson's army down the St. Lawrence against Montreal in a flotilla of small boats. This operation was undertaken in conjunction with a second advance against that city by Major General Wade Hampton's army from the Lake Champlain area. Wilkinson's offensive came to grief on 11 November 1813 when a British shadowing force roughly handled his army at the battle of Crysler's Farm, near present-day Morrisburg, Ontario. News that Hampton had met defeat in a similar action at Chateauguay on 26 October gave the American commander (never an enthusiastic soldier) a welcome chance to cancel operations and go into winter quarters at French Mills, across the St. Lawrence from Cornwall.

Further west, the United States enjoyed success. Major General William Henry Harrison had established a forward base at Fort Meigs on the Maumee River near Lake Erie, and gradually built up his strength. In May and July 1813 he fought off two British sieges and when his naval counterpart, Commander Oliver Hazard Perry, captured the British Lake Erie squadron at Put-In Bay on 10 September 1813, Harrison invaded Canada. Catching up with the retreating British army at the Thames River on 5 October, Harrison dispersed the British force in less than thirty minutes. Sending part of his army back to Detroit (now in American hands again) Harrison moved on to Fort George.

He arrived there on 30 October 1813 to find the post under the command of New York Brigadier General George McClure. The two officers planned a joint attack on Burlington Bay, but before they could put it into effect, Harrison was ordered to Sackets Harbor. By this time, any sympathy that the local population might have had for the Americans had been dissipated by Willcocks who, appointed "police officer" of the Niagara by McClure, had unleashed a reign of terror on any loyal Canadian within reach. Riding at the head of his renegade "Canadian Volunteers," Willcocks gathered intelligence from sympathizers, looted or destroyed property, and arrested prominent loyalists throughout the Niagara area.[11]

As his militiamen's terms of enlistment began to expire and they drifted away, McClure became desperate. By 10 December, only four hundred were left and, on that day, one of Willcocks's patrols was ambushed by British native warriors, losing one killed and four taken prisoner. Panic broke out, both in the American garrison and their commander. Although McClure had instructions from Washington to burn Newark only if it was necessary for the defence of Fort George, he decided to destroy the village and then withdraw across the river. The inhabitants were given twelve hours notice to remove themselves and their property, and then Willcocks, a former resident, and his men put Newark to the torch. An American officer remembered the renegade leader leading "a banditti through the town … setting fire to his neighbour's dwelling" and "applying the epithet of Tory to all who disapproved of this flagrant act of barbarity."[12] By morning, the pretty little community of eighty structures, one of the oldest settlements in Upper Canada, was reduced to smoking ruins.

Enraged, Lieutenant General Gordon Drummond, the British commander in Upper Canada, decided to retaliate. On 19 December, a British force captured Fort Niagara in a daring night raid, and in the weeks that followed, Drummond's subordinate, Major General Phineas Riall (pronounced Ry-all), brushed aside the weak resistance put up by the New York militia, and burned all habitation between Buffalo and Lewiston.

Aghast at the destruction, New York Governor Daniel D. Tompkins requested federal troops to protect the northern border of his state. In response, Armstrong ordered Major General Jacob Brown to march with a small division of troops from French Mills to Sackets Harbor. Arriving there in early February 1814, Brown found confusing instructions from the secretary. He was directed to make an attack over the frozen St. Lawrence against Kingston but, to mask this purpose, he was to use a second (false) set of orders from Armstrong that ordered him to march westward and besiege Fort Niagara. As a recent thaw had made an attack over the ice against Kingston impossible, Brown construed the second set of orders to be his true directions and set out for the Niagara. After considerable confusion and communication with Washington, and much marching and counter-marching, he arrived at Buffalo in early April 1814 and began to plan an offensive against Canada.

By this time, Madison and his cabinet were facing a crisis. They had agreed to enter into peace negotiations with the British government but it would be some time before these talks would begin. Meanwhile, the war in Europe against Napoleon had ended enabling Britain to send massive reinforcements to North America. The United States needed military success to give their negotiators a better bargaining position and it had to come soon. The cabinet, therefore, planned a campaign based on American control of Lake Erie, which allowed the United States to dominate the western theatre. The government ordered the Lake Erie naval squadron to transport an army to recapture the strategically important post of Mackinac.

Diverting these ships, however, frustrated Brown's plan to invade Upper Canada by way of Lake Erie and, on Armstrong's suggestion, he decided on a smaller and more limited operation. He would cross the Niagara River from Buffalo and move north along the Canadian side of the river to Lake Ontario where he would meet with the American squadron on that lake. From there, he could move either on York, Burlington Bay or Kingston.

In the misty early hours of 3 July 1814, Brown's troops marched from their camp and embarked in a flotilla of small boats to cross the Niagara River. The stage was set for the battle of Chippawa ...

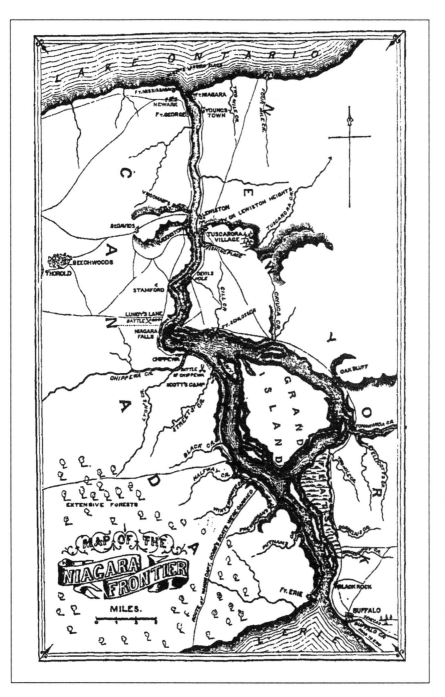

Map 1
The Niagara Frontier, 1814
Map from Benson Lossing, *Pictorial Field Book of the War of 1812*, New York, 1869

Fort Niagara, from Fort George
Strategically located at the mouth of the Niagara River, this fort was taken by
the British in December 1813. The American desire to recapture it was one of
the catalysts of the Niagara campaign of 1814.
From Benson J. Lossing, *Pictorial Field Book of the War of 1812*, New York, 1869

**Lieutenant General Sir George
Prevost, British Army (1767-1816)**
An excellent administrator with a
long military career in the West
Indies and North America, Prevost
was cool, controlled, and cautious.
He followed a defensive strategy
throughout the war, but his ven-
tures into the field at Sackets
Harbor in 1813 and Plattsburgh in
1814 ended badly and blighted
what was otherwise a successful performance in a very difficult position.
Courtesy Chateau Ramezay Museum, Montreal

American Attack on Fort George,
27 May 1813
Following the capture of this post in a near textbook operation, an American army occupied Canadian soil for seven months. This discouraged loyal Canadians but encouraged those not so loyal, such as Joseph Willcocks and his followers, to join the American cause. In December 1813, on American orders, Willcocks and his renegades would burn the little town of Newark, whose church spires are shown in this view, to the ground.
From an engraving in the *Portfolio*, published 1817

Sackets Harbor in 1815
The best anchorage on the American side of Lake Ontario, by 1815 the little village of Sackets Harbor in upstate New York had become the largest military and naval base in the United States. In May 1813, Major General Jacob Brown, who was to command the American army at Chippawa, played a prominent role in successfully defending it against a British attack led by Sir George Prevost. The following October, Sackets Harbor was the launching point for the sixth American invasion of Upper Canada.
From Benson J. Lossing, *Pictorial Field Book of the War of 1812*, New York, 1869, after an engraving in the *Portfolio*, 1815

Major General James Wilkinson,
U.S. Army (1757-1825)
Wilkinson had a distinguished career
in the Continental Army and was the
senior officer of the regular army for
much of the period leading up to the
war. He performed badly during the
War of 1812 and acquired the dubious reputation of never winning a
battle but never losing a court martial
of which he experienced several in
his long and colourful career.

From Benson J. Lossing, *Pictorial Field Book of the
War of 1812*, New York, 1869

Major General Henry Dearborn,
U.S. Army (1751-1829)
Senior officer of the U.S. army at the
outbreak of war, the aging Dearborn
lacked aggressive qualities and was
superseded in the summer of 1813. A
kindly man, he was known to his subordinates as "Granny."

From Benson J. Lossing, *Pictorial Field Book of the
War of 1812*, New York, 1869

A View of Fort George from Fort Niagara, 1813
Constructed in the late 1790s, Fort George commanded the American Fort
Niagara opposite and was the northern anchor of the British defences along the
Niagara River. Captured by Dearborn in May 1813, it was abandoned the fol-
lowing December by New York Brigadier General George McClure, who with-
drew across the river to Fort Niagara.
Painting by Edward Walsh, courtesy National Archives of Canada, C-000026

President James Madison
Fourth president of the United States
(1809-1817), Madison chose war to
resolve his nation's differences with
Great Britain, plunging the republic
into a conflict for which it was manifestly unprepared.
From Benson J. Lossing, *Pictorial Field Book of the
War of 1812*, New York, 1869

Brigadier General William Hull,
U.S. Army (1753-1825)
A veteran of the Revolutionary War,
Hull proved indecisive and incompe-
tent during the War of 1812. After a
half-hearted invasion of Canada he
surrendered Detroit and his army to a
weaker British force commanded by
the aggressive British General Isaac
Brock. Hull's son, Captain Abraham
Hull, fought at Chippawa and was
later killed at the battle of Lundy's
Lane in 1814.

From Benson J. Lossing, *Pictorial Field Book of the
War of 1812*, New York, 1869

Tecumseh (c. 1768-1813)
A chief of the Shawnee, Tecumseh
was an intelligent and charismatic
leader who formed a confederacy of
northwestern native nations. He
allied his people with the British, but
his death at the battle of the Thames
in October 1813 doomed his dream
of an independent native state in
North America.

From Benson J. Lossing, *Pictorial Field Book of the
War of 1812, New York*, 1869

Major General Sir Isaac Brock,
British Army (1769-1812)
British commander in Upper Canada
at the outbreak of war, the competent
and aggressive Brock rebuffed two
American invasions of the province in
1812 at Detroit in August and
Queenston Heights in October.
Unfortunately for Upper Canada, he
was killed during the latter action and
his successors did not prove to be
leaders of the same high calibre.
Watercolour by J. Hudson, courtesy National Archives
of Canada, C-011222

The Battle of Queenston Heights, 13 October 1812
A dramatic modern rendering of the major action of the battle. The British vic-
tory at Queenston Heights brought the second American invasion of Upper
Canada to an abrupt end. Lieutenant Colonel Winfield Scott, U.S. Artillery,
played a major role in this battle; he would later fight at Chippawa.
Painting by John Kelly, courtesy National Archives of Canada, C-000273

York in 1813

Dearborn's capture of York (present-day Toronto), the capital of Upper
Canada, in April 1813 marked the beginning of the fourth American invasion of
Upper Canada during the war. In August 1813, Colonel Winfield Scott was to
capture York in an amphibious raid.

From Benson J. Lossing, *Pictorial Field Book of the War of 1812*, New York, 1869

CHAPTER 2

"GREY JACKETS"
The Left Division, United States Army

The American army that entered Canada in July 1814 was the best military formation the United States was to field during the war. Its high quality was the result of hard lessons learned during the past two years, for the republic had been totally unprepared for war in 1812. The small peacetime army of two regiments of artillery, one regiment of light dragoons, and seven of infantry was not strong enough to conquer Canada, so President James Madison and his cabinet had set about raising an entirely new wartime force (two regiments of artillery, a second regiment of light dragoons, and eighteen regiments of infantry). Ignoring wise advice to mix prewar and wartime regulars in the same units, the Secretary of War in 1812, William Eustis, instead left most of the peacetime regiments in their garrisons – only one, the Fourth Infantry, was sent north, and it was surrendered by Brigadier General William Hull at Detroit in August 1812. The result was that the United States tried to conduct military operations on its northern frontier – a difficult theatre of war - with its vast distances, poor communications, inclement weather, and short campaign seasons – using hastily-recruited and poorly-trained troops who were regular in name only.

Given time and energy, almost everything necessary for an army – recruits, arms, and training – might have been accomplished, but good leadership could not be extemporized. Not enough senior officers were available in the peacetime force so the government had to look elsewhere and there was limited material at hand. Of the seventeen generals appointed in 1812, seven were prewar regular officers and fifteen of the total had revolutionary or militia backgrounds; but, at an average age of fifty-five, they did not inspire confidence.[1]

There were similar problems with the more junior ranks. In 1812, there were only twenty-nine officers of the rank of colonel in the regular army, insufficient for the army of twenty-five thousand men authorized by

Congress in January of that year. Furthermore, the military academy at West Point had not graduated enough officers to fill the vacancies in these new units. Of the 119 graduates of West Point between 1802 and 1815, 101 actually served in the conflict, but only one reached general officer rank during the war. The only solution was to appoint officers from civilian life and the result was, as one commentator remarked, that "men of no talents" procured "some friends to recommend them to members of congress who bring them forward without any other knowledge of them."[2] Commissions were issued at an astonishing rate, eleven hundred in 1812 alone and they came very fast. Isaac Roach of Philadelphia applied for a commission in mid-June – by 2 July, with almost no previous military experience, he was a captain of artillery.[3]

Hastily raised and indifferently officered, the U.S. army on the northern frontier barely survived its first campaigns in 1812. There was a distinct improvement the following year as it began to learn its business. Promotions were made on merit, not political connections; and a new generation of younger, more competent generals came to the fore.

Much emphasis was put on the preparation of troops for battle in 1813 and intensive training was carried out at camps of instruction at Burlington, Vermont, Fort George, Fort Niagara, and Fort Meigs. "We are making such progress," one officer dryly remarked in the spring, "that we shall Die with some grace next summer."[4] The results were apparent, as American regulars performed better at the battles of York, Fort George, Sackets Harbor, and Stoney Creek. But they still proved incapable of defeating British regulars in open battle as the events of Crysler's Farm (where a British force of about one thousand beat off an American army twice its number) conclusively demonstrated.

Nonetheless, the officers and men who had marched into Buffalo with Major General Jacob Brown in April 1814 were far from being raw recruits – most had at least one battle or campaign behind them. They were fortunate in their senior officers for the Left Division, as Brown termed his command, was led by some of the most able men in the wartime American army.[5]

Although he fought and won more pitched battles against British regulars than any other American general, Jacob Jennings Brown is nearly forgotten today. Thirty-nine-years-old in 1814, Brown was one of the few American military leaders to have made a successful transition from the state militia to the regular army. Acting as a surveyor, magistrate, engineer, land agent, realtor, and militia officer, this native of Pennsylvania had laboured for twelve years before opening up the Black River of upper New York state for settlement.

At the outbreak of war, Brown was appointed to command the St. Lawrence frontier. He rebuffed a British attack on Ogdensburg in November 1812 and took a prominent part in the successful defence of Sackets Harbor in May 1813. Commissioned a brigadier general in the regular service, he had a good record during the abortive St. Lawrence campaign of the autumn of 1813, gaining promotion to major general and command of the Left Division in the spring of 1814. Brown was a natural leader – as one observer remarked, he possessed

> all the materials of a Great General united in a very high degree. He is a man of indefatigable perseverance and activity, enterprizing, vigilant, and brave almost to a fault; full of stratagem, fertile in resources, and never disheartened – last but not least, he has that strong and healthy constitution, which enables him at all times to bring the powers of his mind and body to act with the highest vigor.[6]

Brown's ignorance of the formal aspects of the military profession were more than compensated for by twenty-eight-year-old Winfield Scott, the aggressive commander of his First Brigade. Six feet, five inches tall, and every inch ramrod straight, the Virginian Scott was fortune's child. Beginning the war as a captain, he moved steadily upward in rank. Captured at Queenston Heights, he was released from captivity on exchange in 1813 and had planned the attack on Fort George and commanded an amphibious raid on York in August of that year. His abilities and record made Scott one of the leading personalities of the frontier army. He also had an exhaustive knowledge of the technical details of his profession, which he expanded during his leisure hours by studying the contents of a five-foot portable book shelf crammed with European military texts.[7]

The commander of Brown's second brigade of regulars was thirty-two-year-old Brigadier General Eleazar Wheelock Ripley. A native of Massachusetts and a prewar lawyer and state politician, Ripley was cool and controlled. One of the few prominent New Englanders to support the war, Ripley had been commissioned a lieutenant colonel from civilian life in 1812 and had been given command of the Twenty-First Infantry. He proved to be an excellent regimental commander and had turned the Twenty-First into a model unit.[8]

The final general officer in the division was forty-one-year-old New York Brigadier General Peter Buell Porter. A resident of Black Rock and a successful partner in the Porter, Barton company that operated the portage road on the American side of the Niagara, Porter had been elected to

Congress in 1808 and was a leading member of the "war hawk" faction. After serving in the Niagara in 1813, Porter was appointed to command Brown's Third Brigade consisting of volunteer militia from New York and Pennsylvania as well as Willcocks's renegades. The cheerful and efficient Porter had many friends and few enemies.[9]

When Brown's troops arrived at Buffalo in mid-April 1814, they erected a camp on a site near the village chosen by Scott. Situated at Flint Hill near the shore of Lake Erie, this camp offered good water and drainage, cooling breezes, and space for large formations to manoeuvre. Brown did not stay long, as he was forced to return to Sackets Harbor when it, the most important American base on Lake Ontario, came under threat of a British attack. He turned over command to Scott and directed him to prepare the division for the field.

This Scott did with a vengeance. When the snow melted in late April, the Left Division commenced the most vigorous and effective training program experienced by American soldiers during the war. Weather permitting, units drilled between seven and ten hours a day. There were frequent inspections, mock battles, and blank firing exercises. Captain Benjamin Ropes of the Twenty-First Infantry who will be met frequently below and who, the reader must be warned, was an atrocious speller, recorded an average day at Flint Hill:

> ... at Revelee which was at day light, thee Whole Armey were on Drill, except What ware on Guard, they Driled from that time untill Seven Oclock, when they ware Dismissed for Refreshment, at Nine Oclock the whole Ware on Parade, Guards turned of[f], & Troops Dismised, at 10 Oclock, the whole of the Troops aut again to Drill till 12 Oclock, by Companies, Troops dismised for Dinner, at 2 Oclock, again the whole out for Drill, by Regimets, Brigades, & Divesision, Drill till 5 Oclock, at 6 Oclock the Commissioned Officers, dril the Non Commissioned Officers, one hour, & at Sunsett, the whole Army out for evening rool call, in Adition to this, Guard, Police, & washing Duty.[10]

Scott was relentless. He paid scrupulous attention to camp hygiene and sanitation; soldiers were ordered to bathe weekly under an officer's supervision and were to keep their hair, persons, and uniforms neat and tidy. Discipline was strict – a general court martial in May convicted five men of desertion and four were shot by firing squad in front of the assembled brigade. Officers were not exempt from punishment – at one point, of the twenty-six soldiers under arrest, ten held commissions. No detail was small enough to escape the tall general's scrutiny; he regulated exactly the contents of his men's knapsacks – "to which a brush and pocket handkerchief may be added but nothing else."[11]

As many of his men were dressed in rags, Scott spent considerable effort on getting them proper clothing. Drummer Jarvis Hanks of the Eleventh Infantry, for example, boasted a strange pair of trousers he had tailored for himself out of a spare blanket. After much correspondence, Scott discovered that the annual uniform issue for his units had been sent to Plattsburg where it had been expropriated by Major General James Wilkinson for his troops. He pursued the matter until, finally, a shipment of new uniforms arrived at Flint Hill. Instead of the regulation dark blue short-tailed coatee, however, the men received single-breasted, grey woolen jackets, usually worn as a fatigue dress or as an undergarment in winter. But Scott did not care what his men wore as long as they were properly, and uniformly, clad. All stocks of blue coatees were given to the Twenty-First Infantry; the other regiments got the grey jackets. They would make this simple garment famous.[12]

By May the intensive training was showing results, and Scott boasted to a friend:

> I have a handsome little army ... I am most partial to
> these regiments. The men are healthy, sober, cheerful and
> docile. The field officers highly respectable, and many of
> the platoon officers are decent and emulous of improve-
> ment. If, of such material, I do not make the best army
> now in service, by the 1st of June, I will agree to be dis-
> missed [from] the service.[13]

The division began to fill out as new units arrived, eventually consisting of two brigades of regular infantry and one brigade of militia, with attached artillery and cavalry. Scott's thirteen-hundred-strong First Brigade comprised the Ninth, Eleventh, and Twenty-Fifth Infantry. Ripley's Second Brigade, with a total of about one thousand men, consisted of the Twenty-First and Twenty-Third Infantry. Rounding out the regular component of the division were Major Jacob Hindman's battalion of artillery with 327 men, and Captain Samuel Harris's troop of light dragoons, seventy-strong, which only joined the division as it crossed the Niagara River. The artillery consisted of four companies: two with light 6-pdr. field pieces commanded by Captains Nathan Towson and John Ritchie, one with medium 12-pdr.

field pieces commanded by Captain Thomas Biddle, and one with heavy 18-pdr. pieces commanded by Captain Alexander Williams. There was also an artillery reserve of heavy guns and mortars.

Porter's Third Brigade was still in the process of organizing and only one of its units, Colonel James Fenton's Fifth Regiment of Pennsylvania Volunteers, was ready by 3 July. Formed of six-month volunteers and state militia drafts, this 750-strong regiment was drawn from Cumberland, Franklin, and Adams counties, Pennsylvania. Attached to Porter's brigade was a large force of native warriors, between four and five hundred strong, from a variety of nations: Seneca, Allegany, Cattaraugus, Onondaga, Tuscarora, Delaware, Tonawanda, and Stockbridge. They were under the command of New York Lieutenant Colonel Erastus Granger and the Seneca chief, Red Jacket. Overall, Brown was able to deploy about thirty-five hundred regulars, non-regulars, and warriors in the first week of July 1814.[14]

Little is known about the private soldiers of the division. Beyond the official military records, only three personal memoirs by non-commissioned personnel of the Left Division have come to light – written by Drummer Hanks of the Eleventh Infantry, Private Amasiah Ford of the Twenty-Third and Private Alexander McMullen of Fenton's regiment. Jarvis Hanks was an adventurous thirteen-year-old when an army recruiting party visited his village of Pawlet, Vermont, in the spring of 1813. His soft-hearted parents let the lad enlist on the promise that he would not serve in battle – Jarvis was a veteran of four pitched battles before he was fifteen. After a family council, Alexander McMullen volunteered to serve for six months in place of his younger brother, who had been drafted into the militia but was considered too delicate. Private Ford, a seventeen-year-old from Ballston Spa, New York, never recorded why he decided to join the army in February 1813.[15]

Economic pressure, not patriotism, was probably the prime force behind most enlistments. The majority of recruits described their civilian occupations as either "farmers" or "labourers," but those calling themselves "farmers" were most likely itinerant agricultural labourers as opposed to landholders. Such men, vulnerable to economic downturns, enlisted as an alternative to poverty. Certainly, the pay was little incentive – a private in 1814 received eight dollars a month, when he got it; remuneration well below that of less dangerous occupations.[16]

Analyses of the official records show that 86.8 percent of the enlisted personnel in the army were native-born Americans. On average the soldiers in the Left Division were about twenty-five years of age, stood between five feet, seven inches and five feet, eight inches tall, and were more likely to have brown hair than any other colour.[17]

Enlisted men at Buffalo had little free time, as their day was taken up with incessant drills or fatigues. Mealtimes were the high point of the day, and according to Hanks and McMullen the rations were good. By regulation, each man was to receive daily one and a quarter pounds of beef or three quarters of a pound of pork, eighteen ounces of bread, and a due proportion of salt, soap, vinegar, and candles. If he had any money, and he most likely did not, civilian merchants (called "sutlers") would be glad to sell him such delicacies as coffee, tea, sugar or chocolate at high prices. There was also a liquor ration of four ounces of whisky, rum or brandy and, again, the sutler would sell him more at exorbitant prices.[18]

The soldiers of the Left Division wore a uniform designed for every reason but comfort. In Scott's First Brigade, an infantry private wore the single-breasted grey jacket with a collar that came up to his ears, and white cotton trousers rolled above his laced shoes and worn over black gaiters. Headgear consisted of a high, heavy, leather shako, a most uncomfortable and impracticable item easily dislodged by quick movement. The crowning indignity was the stock, a band of stiff leather tied tightly around the neck that forced the wearer to keep his chin up and limited the movement of his head.

Once dressed, the private put on his load-carrying equipment, which consisted of a black leather cartouche, with forty rounds of ball cartridge, worn on the right hip and secured by a wide buff or black leather belt over the left shoulder. A similar belt over the right shoulder carried the bayonet in its scabbard on the soldier's left hip. These two shoulder belts met on the man's chest to give a "cross belt" effect. Over the cross belts went straps for the soldier's canteen (a miniature wooden barrel) and his haversack (a white cloth ration bag). These two last items were usually worn on the left hip. Over all this went the chest and shoulder harness for the knapsack worn on the soldier's back, which contained his uniforms and personal items, with his blanket rolled tightly and secured on top. Finally, dressed and equipped, the typical private was ready to pick up his Springfield musket.[19]

By late June, many of the men at Buffalo had been drilling for nearly ten weeks and, in Scott's words, were beginning "to sigh for orders to beat up the enemy's quarters" as a means of relief.[20] The division was in high spirits. Major Thomas Jesup of the Twenty-Fifth Infantry recorded that the officers had decided, as point of honour, "to go into action with sashes and epaulettes, and to wear … every thing our country allowed us to wear."[21] For Drummer Hanks, the ruined village of Buffalo had given him and his comrades "feelings of deep sympathy" for the inhabitants and "sharpened up our courage to prepare for effectual retribution when we should enter Canada upon the anticipated campaign."[22] On 2 July 1814 when the long-awaited announcement came that the Left Division would invade Canada that night, it was ready and eager to go.

Brigadier General Peter B. Porter,
New York Militia (1773-1844)
The easygoing Porter, a born politician, was a prewar member of congress and a prominent member of the
"war hawk" faction that agitated for a
military solution to the problems
between the United States and Great
Britain. As a militia general, Porter
participated in the 1813 campaign in
the Niagara and commanded the
Third Brigade of Brown's Left
Division during the 1814 campaign.
Courtesy Buffalo and Erie County Historical Society,
C-19269

Buffalo in 1813
In retaliation for the American burning of the Canadian village of Newark in
December 1813, British troops razed the American side of the Niagara. When
Brown's army established a camp at Buffalo in the spring of 1814 the pretty little
village was little more than a collection of chimneys and a few temporary
shacks.
From Benson Lossing, *Pictorial Field Book of the War of 1812*, New York, 1869

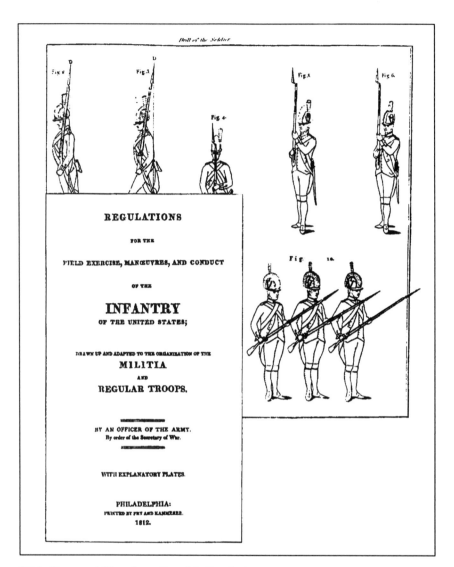

Title Page and Plate from Smyth's *Regulations,* 1812

As there was a controversy within the American army over the standard manual in use, Winfield Scott chose this work as the basis for the training of the Left Division in the camp at Flint Hill in the spring of 1814. A direct abridgement of the 1792 French *Règlement* for infantry, the figures in the plate show the manual's heritage as they are portrayed wearing French uniforms.

Courtesy Frederick P. Gaede

Winfield Scott Training the Left Division
A woodcut depicting the tall figure of Scott instructing at the camp at Flint Hill.
From April to June 1814, Scott provided a collection of ragged but veteran
troops with the most intense and effective training American soldiers received
during the war – the results of his efforts would be evident at Chippawa. The
uniforms portrayed are incorrect as they are those of the early 1840s.
From David Strother, *An Illustrated Life of General Winfield Scott*, New York, 1847

U.S. Artilleryman, 1813-1814
Throughout the war, the artillery regiments were the best-led and best-disciplined troops in the American army. This gunner wears a blue coatee (or short-tailed coat) with red collar and cuffs, yellow braid, and brass buttons. Major Jacob Hindman's battalion of artillery that served at Chippawa may have worn a similar uniform.

Painting by H.C. McBarron, courtesy Parks Canada

U.S. Infantry Sergeant and Private, 1814

Depicted wearing the regulation blue short-tailed coatee with white trim – the uniform that Winfield Scott tried but failed to obtain for his troops. The sergeant's rank (see the figure on the left) was designated by two white wool epaulettes, red sash, and sword. Both soldiers have a pricker and brush, used to clean their musket vents and pans after repeated firing, attached to their cross-belts. The enlisted men of the Left Division were more likely to have joined the army for economic, rather than patriotic, reasons.

Drawing by G.A. Embleton, courtesy of the artist

U.S. Light Dragoon, 1814
Dressed in a dark blue jacket, white buckskin breeches, and a leather helmet festooned with a white horsehair fall, the American cavalryman had a splendid appearance but his effectiveness in Canada was limited, as the local terrain was not conducive to this mobile arm.
Painting by H.C. McBarron, courtesy Parks Canada

Brigadier General Winfield Scott,
U.S. Army (1786-1866)
Twenty-eight years old, six feet, five
inches tall, with a stern visage, deep
chest, and booming voice, Scott
looked the "Perfect God of War." He
was a professional soldier who provided the intensive training that made
Brown's Left Division a potent fighting
force. He was to remain in active service until 1861 and dominated the
nineteenth-century American army.
Courtesy National Portrait Gallery, Smithsonian
Institution, Negative 07910

U.S. Infantry Officer, 1814
His rank denominated by two silver metal epaulettes, a red sash, and a sword,
this officer wears a dark blue coatee with white overalls strapped under his
boots. The use of rolled blanket, rather than a knapsack, to carry personal possessions was common during this period, and the officers of Scott's First Brigade
at Chippawa would have had a similar appearance. By 1814, the incompetents
of the first two years of war had been weeded out, and the junior leaders of the
Left Division were tough and experienced veterans.
Drawing by G.A. Embleton, courtesy of the artist

Porter's Residence on the Niagara River at Black Rock
A prosperous merchant and congressman, Porter agitated for war against Great
Britain. As he resided within artillery range of the British Fort Erie, Porter might
have been more circumspect. In November 1812, a round shot went through his
house while Porter was having dinner, an indication of British and Canadian
attitudes toward his political stance.
From Benson Lossing, *Pictorial Field Book of the War of 1812*, New York, 1869

**Major General Jacob Brown,
U.S. Army (1775-1828)**
Although he fought and won more
pitched battles against British regular troops than any other American
general in two wars, Brown is almost
forgotten today. A New York militia
officer with a reputation as a fighter,
he was brought into the regular
army in 1813 and promoted major
general and commander of the Left
Division in 1814. During the following summer, he conclusively demonstrated that well-led and trained
American regulars were capable of
beating a professional foe in open
battle.
Portrait by James Herring after an original by John
Wesley Jarvis. Courtesy New York Historical
Society, Neg. No. 6384

Red Jacket (c. 1750-1830)
A Seneca war chief from western
New York, Red Jacket was one of
the leaders of the native force that
served with Porter's Third Brigade
during the campaign of 1814. At
Chippawa, the native warriors of
both sides fought a violent battle in
which no quarter was asked and
none was given.
From Benson Lossing, *Pictorial Field Book of the War of 1812*, New York, 1869

Infantryman, Scott's
Brigade, 1814
Although he tried to obtain
the proper uniforms for his
brigade during the spring of
1814, Scott was forced to
accept grey jackets, usually
worn as an undergarment or
for fatigues, instead of the
regulation short-tailed blue
coatee. His men would make
this humble garment famous.
Painting by Don Troiani, Southbury,
Ct., U.S.A., based on research by
James L. Kochan

CHAPTER 3

"RED COATS"
The Right Division,
British Army in North America

Waiting on the Canadian side of the river were Major General Phineas Riall and the Right Division of the British army. Thirty-nine years old in the summer of 1814, the Anglo-Irish Riall was a short, rather stout man with an impatient temperament. He had entered the army at the age of nineteen in 1794 to experience a rapid rise in rank through the purchase system – at age twenty-four, he was a lieutenant colonel. By the summer of 1813, when he was sent to North America, Riall was a major general.[1]

Despite his lengthy career, Riall had seen relatively little active service, commanding an infantry battalion in the West Indies in 1805 and, four years later, a brigade in the attack on Martinique. Most recently, he had commanded the campaign of retribution against the American side of the Niagara in December 1813.

A division in name only, Riall's Right Division was scattered in small detachments at York, Burlington Bay, and along the length of the Niagara. Riall worried that his flanks on Lakes Ontario and Erie were vulnerable and requested permission from his superior, Lieutenant General Gordon Drummond, to pull most of his forces back from the Niagara to some central point where he could move to any threatened point. Drummond, however, was adamant that Riall stay on the river, lest the Canadian side of the Niagara suffer from "outrages" similar to those carried out by Joseph Willcocks the previous year.[2]

Ordered to hold in place, Riall put the Niagara region in the best state of defence he could, but throughout the spring of 1814 he deluged his superiors with dire warnings of the consequences if he was not reinforced. The number and intensity of these alarming missals, coupled with fall-out from ongoing feuds between Riall and his artillery and engineer officers, led

Sir George Prevost to consider replacing him. Following a strong endorsement by Drummond, dated 2 July, the day the Americans crossed the Niagara, the Irishman was left in command.[3]

In the first week of July 1814, Riall had about 2700 troops stationed along the thirty-mile length of the Canadian side of the river. His main strength was in the forts at the river mouth: the 100th Regiment of Foot at Fort Niagara and the 1st Foot at Fort George. Detachments of infantry were also stationed at Queenston, Chippawa, and Fort Erie. Dispersed among these garrisons were detachments of regular and militia artillery and cavalry. Riall's third regular infantry unit, the 8th Foot, was on its way back to the Niagara area from York the day the American army crossed the river. The three regular infantry battalions were the backbone of the Right Division and, in this at least, Riall was fortunate as all three were veteran units commanded by experienced and competent officers.[4]

The infantry were supported by Major Robert Lisle's squadron of the 19th Light Dragoons, the only regular cavalry unit to serve in Canada during the war, which had seen service in the Niagara in 1813. Serving with Lisle was Canadian Captain W. Hamilton Merritt's troop of Niagara Light Dragoons, a long-service militia unit whose local knowledge was invaluable.

Riall's artillery consisted of Captain James Maclachlane's company of the Royal Artillery, and this veteran Scot also commanded the detachments of Royal Marine and militia artillery which garrisoned the forts at the river's mouth. His second captain, James Mackonochie, commanded that part of the company formed into a mobile field brigade (or battery) equipped with two 24-pdr. guns, five 6-pdr. guns, and one 5.5 inch howitzer.[5]

Much has been written about the British soldier of the Napoleonic period; and much of it is inaccurate. There is a still-current myth that the army consisted of a brutal and licentious soldiery held in check only by means of harsh discipline inflicted upon them by aristocratic and amateurish officers. Such an impression is false. By 1814, Britain had been at war, with a brief two-year pause, since 1793 and her armed forces, through dint of sheer necessity, had reached a high state of professionalism. This change was largely due to the reforms initiated by the army's commander-in-chief, the Duke of York, in 1796, that left no part of the army – training and promotion, recruiting, discipline, pay, tactical doctrine, weaponry, and organization – untouched.

Most important was reform of the purchase system of promotion. This system, by which British officers literally bought their rank, is often misunderstood. Although it was subject to tremendous abuse, the British government retained it for two reasons. First, as the Crown did not have to provide officers with pensions, the sale of their last commission provided the funds for their retirement. And, second, it was thought that officers who had a financial stake in the stability of the army, and thus the government, would be more loyal to that government.

York's changes to this system precluded a rapid rise in rank such as that enjoyed by Riall. Officers were required to serve a certain time in each rank before being eligible for promotion, and promotion by purchase went by regimental seniority – when a captaincy fell vacant in a regiment, it was offered first to the most senior lieutenant. York also made use of his own patronage to promote penniless officers of ability. The result was that, by 1814, it has been estimated that only one in five promotions were gained through purchase, the remainder by seniority or merit.[6]

Army regulations were not forthcoming on just who could become an officer, stating only that a candidate for a commission be sixteen years of age and have recommendations concerning his "Character, Education, and Bodily Health."[7] In practice, this meant that any literate person was eligible for a commission. As promotion went by regimental seniority, officers stayed with their units for extended periods – the average time in grade of lieutenants in the 1st Foot in 1814, for example, was 4.2 years. In sum, the British army was led by long-service professionals who learned their trade by serving with the troops.[8]

The enlisted personnel of the army were also experienced. Private soldiers signed up for a minimum of seven years and usually remained in the ranks for long periods. For example, in 1814 the average length of service for a soldier in the 8th Foot was between seven and ten years. Although Riall had one infantry battalion from Scotland, one from England, and one from Ireland, most of the enlisted men in all three units were Irish. Casualty statistics of the 1st Foot suffered at Chippawa shows that, of the sixty-two men for whom records of origins exist, exactly half were recruited in Ireland. A similar phenomenon existed in the supposedly English 8th Foot.[9]

In 1814 there was little incentive for anyone to enlist in the British army. The pay was bad (and privates did not receive a pay raise until 1891), rations were not much better, and discipline was harsh in the extreme. Although things were changing, the lash was too often used to punish even the most minor infractions. In the first five months of 1815, thirty-six men of the 8th Foot were tried by regimental court martial for offences ranging from being drunk on duty to attempted desertion. Thirty-four were sentenced to be flogged, the average award being three hundred lashes, although in two-thirds of the cases the punishment was later reduced to a more moderate one or two hundred. Although it may sound barbaric to the modern reader, these punishments were simply a reflection of British society at the time. The criminal code of 1814 listed 225 offences warranting capital punishment – including theft of a sheep or goods worth more than one shilling.[10]

The harshness of army life was no secret, and although recruiting sergeants occasionally picked up the odd recruit who joined out of patriotism, the vast majority of men enlisted because of economic duress. This was especially true in those areas of the British Isles, such as the Midlands, where industrialization was creating sizable numbers of unemployed. George Ferguson of Dublin, a married clerk with one child, had fallen on such bad times that enlistment was the only way he could feed his family. Ferguson's wife and child accompanied him throughout his military service as did the dependents of many common soldiers. The 8th Foot alone reported sixty-six women and seventy-four children with the unit at the end of the war.[11]

In age and appearance, the average infantryman of the Right Division was between twenty-six and twenty-eight years old and from five foot, six inches to five foot, seven inches tall. He wore a thick red wool uniform coatee or short-tailed jacket, and a tall false-fronted shako of black felt. Regiments in the army were distinguished by the metal of their buttons, the shape and pattern of the lace or trim on the front of their coatees, and by the colour of the garment's collar and cuffs – blue for the 1st and 8th Foot, deep yellow for the 100th. The soldier's load-carrying equipment and its attendant straps were similar to those of his American counterpart, and like his fellow in the Left Division he, too, suffered from the choking confinement of a leather stock.

Contrasting the regular's ordered existence was the large force of native warriors attached to the Right Division. They were drawn from two distinct groups: members of the western nations who were refugees from the defeat at the Thames the previous October, and warriors of the Grand River nations. In late June 1814, the Grand River contingent remained at their homes until needed while the western braves, mostly Ottawas, Chippawas, Munseys and Delawares, but including men from the Saukies, Fox, Shawnee, Kickapoo, and Wyandot nations, were split between camps at Fort George and Burlington Bay. A select force from both groups, three hundred strong, was camped near the falls of Niagara under the command of Captain John Norton, a Mohawk war chief of mixed parentage, and after Tecumseh, the most effective native leader on the British side during the war.[12]

Riall did not place much confidence in the last part of his command – the sedentary militia of the Niagara region. The laws of Upper Canada stipulated that every male between the ages of sixteen and fifty had to serve in the militia and turn out for service when called. The sedentary militia (ordered out as required as opposed to militia units embodied for a longer period) was organized into regiments by county and companies by locality. No British officer really counted on these men to replace regular troops in battle, but they rendered an essential service as labourers, lines of communication troops, and sentries.

Riall could call on the immediate services of the 1st and 2nd Lincoln Regiments whose unit areas ran along the Canadian side of the Niagara. For sedentary militia, the Lincolns were fairly experienced, having been called out many times during the previous two years. But they were weak in numbers: the 1st Lincoln from the area around Newark and Fort George possessed only six companies with 399 officers and men, while the 2nd Lincoln, whose territory ran from Queenston to Chippawa, had 416 men in ten companies – but only ninety-five muskets.[13]

Riall did not rely too much on the militia but placed his trust in the quality of his regulars, who were tough and dangerous opponents. An army of trained professionals, well-officered at the regimental level and below, its men had beaten American soldiers many times. As Lieutenant William MacEwen of the Royal Scots expressed it, when fighting the Americans, "we have always been the victorious party."[14] Sergeant James Commins of the 8th Foot summarized the regulars' confidence when he wrote that: "War was a new game to the Americans" as they "had not seen [a] hostile engagement in the[ir] country for forty years."[15] War was not a new game to the British army.

Commodore Sir James Lucas Yeo, RN
The British naval commander on the Great Lakes, Yeo was more aggressive than his American counterpart, Chauncey. Nonetheless, he was wary about taking his fleet onto the lake when Chauncey was ahead in the "war of carpenters," the naval shipbuilding race that raged throughout the war.
Portrait by A. Buck, 1810, courtesy National Archives of Canada, C-022895

Gunners of the Royal Artillery, Full Dress, 1814
A period print showing two enlisted men of the Royal Regiment of Artillery wearing the full dress uniform in 1814, which was blue coatee, or short-tailed coat, with red collar and cuffs. Note the large cartridge box holding sixty rounds; British infantry carried a similar box in black leather. At Chippawa the efficient and professional Royal Artillery would be matched by their American counterparts.
Courtesy Parks Canada

Officer and Dragoon, 19th Light Dragoons, Full Dress, 1814
The 19th were the only regular British cavalry regiment to serve in Canada during the war and fought at Chippawa. They were armed with both a flintlock carbine and a sabre. Clad in dark blue uniforms with yellow trim, their appearance was, if anything, even more splendid than their American counterparts.
Painting by Charles Stadden, courtesy Parks Canada

British Army Punishment, 1814

Although many officers were averse to flogging as a means of corporal punishment, it was common during the War of 1812. In this modern depiction, the drum-major, the non-commissioned officer tasked with carrying out punishments, watches and counts the strokes as one of his drummers uses the traditional "cat of nine tails" on a poor unfortunate lashed to a triangle of sergeants' halberds.

Painting by Eugene Leliepvre, courtesy Parks Canada

Officer of the British Indian Department, Full Dress, 1814

The Indian Department, responsible for the administration and organization of the various contingents of native warriors, was an important and integral part of the defence of Canada. This officer is depicted wearing the full dress scarlet uniform; on active service, departmental officers wore more comfortable and serviceable garb.

Painting by Charles Stadden, courtesy Parks Canada

British Soldiers Working on a Fatigue Detail

In garrison and in the field, when the British regular was not drilling or campaigning he was often working on fatigue details. These soldiers are depicted wearing the standard fatigue dress of the infantry, the service uniform was too valuable and too scarce in North America to be worn for labour such as this.

Painting by Eugene Leliepvre, courtesy Parks Canada

British Patrol of the War of 1812
Guided by a native scout, three members of the Canadian Voltiguers, a French-speaking unit raised in Lower Canada, undertake a patrol. The warrior is armed with a musket and a combination pipe/tomahawk and wears a practical combination of European and native garb.
Painting by G.A. Embleton, courtesy Parks Canada

Joseph Brant, Chief of the Mohawk Nation
This portrait painted in the 1790s depicts how native warriors may have looked during the War of 1812, wearing a combination of European and traditional clothing. Unlike their white counterparts, they dressed for utility and comfort.
Courtesy National Gallery of Canada, 5777

Royal Artillery Gun Detachment with Brass 6-pdr. Field Gun
Military re-enactors, wearing the service dress of the Royal Artillery, fire a field piece at night. Note the muzzle blast, flaming combustive material and sparks, that often set fire to the surrounding grass in dry weather. Captain James Mackonochie's gunners manned three 6-pdr. guns similar to this one at the battle of Chippawa in 1814.
Courtesy D.J. Glenney, Parks Canada

Colour Party, British Infantry, 1814
A period print showing the ensign and
colour sergeant of a British infantry
regiment in 1814. The single chevron and
coat of arms insignia on the sergeant's
upper arm is the badge for colour
sergeants. At Chippawa, three sets of
regimental colours, from the 1st, 8th and
100th Foot, were carried into battle.
Courtesy Parks Canada.

British Light Infantry Officer's Sabre, War of 1812
Although he used it as rarely in combat as the soldier did his bayonet, the sword
was the combat officer's badge of office and almost always worn on duty. Note
the lion's head pommel, a decorative feature as common on British swords of
this period as the eagle was on American edged weapons.
Courtesy Parks Canada

British Private, 1st Regiment of Foot, Service Dress, 1814
During the war the rank and file of the British line infantry regiments serving in North America wore similar brick red, wool coatee (or short-tailed coat). Individual units were distinguished by the colour of their collars and cuffs and the shape of the lace adorning the button-holes. The red coats were long-service professionals, well trained, and well led, and constituted a tough opponent for the less experienced American army.
Painting by G.A. Embleton, courtesy Parks Canada

CHAPTER 4

THE TRADE AND ITS TOOLS
Land Warfare in 1814

To the modern reader living in the last decade of a violent century, warfare at the time of Chippawa has a certain quaint air about it, appearing to be a rather formal affair conducted in gentlemanly fashion by armies clad in fantastic and colourful uniforms. Nothing could be further from the truth – combat in the Napoleonic period was the same brutal business it is today, and was in Julius Caesar's time. To comprehend fully what took place on a farm field north of Street's Creek, Upper Canada, on 5 July 1814, and what its participants experienced, it is first necessary to understand the nature of land warfare in 1814.

Although the War of 1812 was a North American conflict, its major campaigns and battles were conducted according to European military practice. Armies of this period consisted of three combat arms – infantry, cavalry and artillery – each having specific tasks in battle. The most numerous and important arm was the infantry, the "Queen of Battles," which, supported by the artillery with firepower and the cavalry by mobility and shock, took ground and held it. As large numbers of cavalry were not deployable in the wooded terrain of North America, the war was largely an infantry conflict.

The infantryman's main weapon was the flintlock, smoothbore musket. The most common British weapon in service was the India Pattern, originally produced for the East India company's native troops, but because of its ease of manufacture and cost, it was introduced into the regular army. The India Pattern measured just over six feet with its bayonet fixed, and weighed ten pounds, eleven ounces. It fired a ball weighing just over an ounce from its .75 calibre (.75 of an inch) bore. The standard U.S. weapon was the 1795 Springfield or one of its later variants. It was about the same size as the India Pattern but had a smaller .69 calibre bore. Issued with his musket was the infantryman's second weapon, a fourteen to sixteen-inch bayonet with a triangular cross-section that locked onto its muzzle.[1]

The musket consisted of three major components: the "lock," the "stock," and the "barrel" (hence the origin of the expression). The iron barrel was fixed to the wooden stock by pins or retaining bands. The most important component was the "lock" or ignition system, which had three main parts: the "cock," the "lock plate," and the "frizzen." The "cock," with a pair of screw-tightened jaws holding the flint, was connected to the trigger by means of an internal lever and mounted on the "lock plate," which was inset into a wooden stock. The "frizzen" was a hinged piece of steel positioned over the "pan," a trough connecting with the bore by means of a "touch-hole."

To load and fire his musket, the soldier first took a cartridge from the leather cartouche on his right hip. This was a tube of strong paper, sealed with thread and containing powder in one end and a soft lead ball or bullet in the other. Holding the weapon horizontally in his left hand, the soldier bit off the end of the cartridge containing the powder, poured some onto the pan and closed the frizzen. Bringing the weapon to the vertical, he jammed the remainder of the charge, the ball, and the paper – in that order – down the muzzle and pushed it to the bottom of the barrel with his ramrod. Removing the ramrod, he then aimed the weapon and pulled the hammer back to full cock. On command, he pulled the trigger, which brought the hammer and flint down, opening the frizzen and striking sparks. The sparks ignited the powder in the pan and, by means of the touch-hole, the charge in the bore. Surprising as it may seem, trained men could get off four to five rounds per minute under practice conditions, but in battle two to three rounds seem to have been about average.[2]

The musket was a tricky weapon with a number of inherent problems. The touch-hole might become clogged with powder residue, the flint might fall from the jaws, in the excitement a man might fire off his ramrod or, not noticing that his weapon had not discharged, load two or three charges with dire results. Wet weather meant damp powder and poor ignition, repeated firing resulted in barrels that were painfully hot to hold, and the smouldering fragments expelled from the muzzle with each round constituted a definite fire hazard. Even if the thing fired well, each round produced a pall of filthy, grey-white smoke, and when hundreds were fired together the result was a choking cloud around the men using them.

Accuracy was quite another matter. The lead ball, often misshapen because of poor casting and because it was considerably smaller than the bore, would careen out the muzzle with its trajectory decided by its last strike on the bore. The weapon had a tendency to fire high, so to hit a target at close range care had to be taken to aim at least a foot below it. What it came down to was that, although the maximum range of the weapon might have been over two hundred yards, a volley was only effective to about one hundred and fifty yards, while an individual marksman would have difficulty hitting a man-size target at a distance over one hundred yards.[3]

If used in numbers, however, the shortcomings of the individual musket – low rate of fire, inaccuracy, and short range – could be overcome. The basis of infantry combat in 1814 was the deployment of units armed with hundreds of muskets against similar units. Contemporary military doctrine laid great stress on the formation and manoeuvring of these units, and emphasized the organization and fire of sub-units within each British infantry battalion or American infantry regiment.

At full strength (which was rarely the case) an American regiment consisted of ten companies. For firing and manoeuvring purposes, these ten companies were further broken down into "platoons," a term used differently in 1814 than it is today. In 1814, it meant an *ad hoc* fire and manoeuvre unit (usually two per company) formed just before battle. With a well-trained regiment organized into such sub-units, a commander could deliver that weight of fire on whatever target he deemed most appropriate: by platoons in sequence, by companies either in sequence or in groups, by divisions (a group of two companies), by wings (a group of five companies) or, if necessary, by every man in the regiment. Thus, the regiment became the weapon, not the individual musket, and the commander directed his fire as he saw fit.

The best formation for delivering musketry was the line, as every man in a battalion or regiment formed in a line of two ranks (a rank is a series of men standing side by side) could bring his weapon to bear. Although the manuals used by both armies stressed that the line should consist of three ranks (and the Left Division was certainly trained in this formation at Flint Hill), both armies seemed to have preferred the two-rank line in action. The reason was simple – beside allowing all the muskets to bear, a unit formed in two ranks covered more ground, and because of the shallow depth of the formation it suffered fewer casualties from artillery fire. Behind the two ranks of combat troops was stationed a third rank of "file closers," junior officers and sergeants, whose job it was to steady the men and move them in toward the centre as casualties were taken. The standard practice was to equalize the strength of the platoons, or firing sub-units, so that if one took heavy casualties its survivors were distributed among the others.

The line formation was less useful for movement, and in 1814 only the British army was partial to it for both fire and movement – a reflection of its excellent state of training. The Left Division was trained to manoeuvre in "column" (either a thickened line of ten to fifteen ranks in depth, or a column of march longer than it was wide), but the Left Division too was capable of manoeuvring in line. No matter what the formation chosen, the deployment and manoeuvre of infantry formations was a fairly elegant and dignified business in 1814, as well it might be given the range and inaccuracy of the weapons in use.[4]

Each infantry battalion or regiment possessed a pair of flags or "colours" that were placed in the centre of its line, in front of the commanding officer in order to mark his position. These devices served as a rallying point and a guide upon which units could maintain their dressing while manoeuvring. Being conspicuous, they attracted fire, making the job of carrying them (usually accorded to the most junior officers) a very hazardous business.

Not all soldiers fought in the ordered formations prescribed by the drill manuals of the two armies. Both divisions contained a portion of men who, either by training or predilection, acted as "light infantry." In this respect Riall was better served as each of his three battalions possessed a trained light infantry company. Although U.S. regulations authorized two light infantry companies in each infantry regiment, there appears to have been no formal organization for such troops in the American army in 1814 – instead, the four regular rifle regiments performed this function. Brown, however, had no rifle units with him at Niagara. He relied, therefore, on his native warriors and militia volunteers for this role, but this met only with partial success.

The function of light infantry was to form the vanguard of an army on the march and the rear guard when retreating. In battle they covered and protected their line infantry by forming a screen of skirmishers that hung on the flanks of an enemy formation, and annoyed it with individually aimed musketry. Light infantrymen usually fought in pairs, one man always with a loaded musket ready to cover his partner, and although they moved more quickly than ordinary infantry, they maintained a loose but controlled formation. It was work that demanded special skills - the ideal light infantryman being described as having "good wind and long endurance ... a correct and ready knowledge of the aspects of ground and position, a mind of enterprise, a bold and daring courage – ardent in pursuit of glory – matured by knowledge and correct estimate of effect in all the variety of circumstance which occur."[5] This was a pretty tall order and not the kind of qualities likely to be found in the average Canadian or American militiaman in 1814.

Besides the light infantry, a British battalion possessed another elite

company, the grenadier, which acted as the battalion's shock unit and consisted of the battalion's most veteran soldiers. When the battalion formed in
line, the grenadiers took position on the right flank while the light infantry
company took post on the left flank. For this reason, the two were often
referred to as the "flank" companies.

The clash of infantry against infantry was the most important aspect of
the Napoleonic battle. A typical action involved the manoeuvre of opposing
formations in line or column, covered by skirmishing light infantry and
supported by artillery. When the formations closed with each other, typical-
ly, one side, its nerve and stamina weakened by artillery fire and short range
musketry, usually gave way, sometimes assisted on its way by the bayonets
of the other. But actual bayonet fighting was rare – it was the threat of that
weapon, not its use, that was important. As one American officer remarked,
the bayonet "is a potent weapon, on the side of high discipline and strong
nerves" but "the charge of the bayonet is not often used."[6] There was, however, another weapon on the 1814 battlefield that was not only feared but
also used – artillery.

Recent technological advances had rendered artillery the most powerful
arm in battle. The main weapon was the gun, basically an elongated metal
cylinder open at the muzzle end. A charge of powder and a projectile were
loaded into the hollow centre or bore of the gun, and when the charge was
ignited the resulting explosion propelled the projectile out the muzzle
toward the target. Guns were designated by the weight of the round shot
they fired; a 12-pdr. (pounder) gun, thus, fired a shot weighing twelve
pounds. The most common and useful gun in the War of 1812 was the
6-pdr., but both sides routinely brought larger types into the field.[7]

Guns fired various projectiles. The most important was round shot,
which in the Royal Artillery composed about seventy to eighty percent of
the ammunition carried. Round shot was simply a solid iron sphere used to
destroy structures and to kill men and horses. The heavier the shot, the
greater its impact velocity – a 12-pdr. shot was about twice as effective on
target as a 3-pdr. shot. Round shot had a fearsome effect – contemporary
tests demonstrated that under optimum conditions a 12-pdr. shot could, at
a range of 600 to 700 yards, penetrate thirty-six human beings or eight feet
of compacted earth, while a 6-pdr. shot could cut through nineteen men or
seven feet of earth.

Canister (or, as the Royal Artillery termed it, case shot) was an anti-personnel round. It was simply a cylindrical tin canister filled with bullets,
which when fired disintegrated, spraying a shower of lead. It has been calculated that a single salvo of canister from a battery of six 6-pdr. guns was
the equivalent of a musketry volley by an entire infantry battalion.

Shrapnel was a projectile used only by the Royal Artillery. It was basically a shell, a thin-walled, hollow iron sphere, filled with gun powder and bullets, and exploded by a fuse. The round was loaded with the fuse resting against the propellant, charge whose flash ignited it and, hopefully, travelled the required distance before exploding. If fired properly, shrapnel was highly effective, but as there was a shortage of this type of projectile in Canada, it was used sparingly.

The other main weapon of the artillery was the howitzer, a short, squat piece that pitched explosive shells or shrapnel on a high trajectory. Both the American and British armies favoured the light 5.5-inch howitzer, a somewhat erratic weapon, but one that fired a fairly heavy projectile for its size. Howitzer shells were similar to shrapnel shells but they contained only powder. Period tests showed that a light howitzer shell, when it burst, disintegrated into twenty to thirty jagged metal shards that frequently flew as far as 250 feet from the bursting point. A useful weapon, one howitzer was usually provided for every five or six guns in the artillery of most nations.

When a battery arrived at its firing position, the pieces were detached from their limbers, the two-wheeled apparatus that converted their carriages into a four-wheeled vehicle. The ammunition was made ready, and the caissons that contained reserve ammunition, including the limbers, were removed to a safe distance. Artillery pieces were usually positioned between thirty-six and sixty feet apart so that they could be traversed (aligned in the horizontal plane) across a broad front, and also to allow the limbers and horse teams to move easily through and around them.

To load the gun, a flannel or serge cartridge (a bag containing the propellant charge) was rammed down the bore, followed by the projectile. The cartridge was "pricked" with a brass wire, pushed down the vent or touch-hole of the piece, and fired by means of a brass tube, filled with powder, that was then placed in the vent, and ignited. Firing was usually by rotation, one gun firing after another. This was done to keep the target under constant fire, to maintain safety in the gun position, to minimize the amount of smoke, and always to keep a loaded weapon should a target of opportunity arise. To preserve ammunition, the rate of fire was kept down – one round per minute for light pieces and a round every two minutes for heavier pieces seems to have been about standard.

As a general rule the maximum range of light guns in 1814 was about one thousand yards, while the range of heavier pieces was about twice that distance. However, the maximum *effective* range of both types was considerably less, and the effective range of howitzers was between eight and nine hundred yards. Different projectiles were fired at different ranges. The British practice was to fire canister at targets within 350 yards range and shrapnel or round shot at targets over that range. The American practice was to fire shot at targets over five to six hundred yards range, and canister below that range.[8]

As artillery could only fire on a target it could see, gun positions had to be chosen with great care. The command of artillery in battle, wrote a French commentator of the time, consists of "the art of positioning it and directing its fire to have the worst possible effect on the enemy and give the greatest protection to the troops which it supports."[9] Generally, during the War of 1812, artillery performed better in the defence than it did in the offence, because not enough guns were deployed in North America to create the massed firepower necessary to destroy opposing infantry. Nonetheless, it has been calculated that, during this period, a well-served artillery piece could inflict an average of one or two casualties for every round fired.[10]

Early nineteenth-century military actions were limited in space. The tactics and the short ranges of the weaponry used in 1814 allowed generals to compress their formations to a degree that is almost unthinkable to the modern soldier. The entire front covered by the three British regular battalions at Chippawa, about thirteen hundred soldiers, would today be covered by about sixty men.[11]

Then as now, the infantry did most of the fighting and took the heaviest casualties. The infantryman's experience of battle in 1814 was truly terrifying. Given the primitive state of military logistics, the soldier often entered combat hungry, and usually tired after a long march. Blinded by powder smoke, packed in tightly crowded ranks, watching round shot bouncing towards him but unable to move, suffering from raging thirst brought on by tension and the necessity of biting into cartridges containing bitter black powder, seeing men killed and maimed around him, the infantryman stood, fought, and died. Not the worst of the business were the unnerving sounds peculiar to battle: the deadly "hissing," "whizzing," "sighing" or "whistling" of passing round shot; the "rattle" of canister bullets on rows of bayonets; the ominous "thud" of musket balls impacting on human flesh, followed by the screams, moans, and pleas of the wounded and dying.

Why didn't men flee? Some did, but most stayed and did so for a number of reasons. Perhaps the most important was the proximity of comrades for, in contrast to their modern counterparts, the soldiers of 1814 could take comfort from the close presence of their fellows. As one remembered: "I looked alongst the line" and the "steady determined scowl of my companions assured my heart and gave me determination."[12] The crowded formations of the period had two important effects – men were reluctant to engage in acts which their comrades would regard as cowardice and, at the same time, their steadiness was buttressed by the knowledge that running would place their comrades and units in danger. Most, making "the cold choice between two alternatives," found that "fixed resolve not to quit; an act of renunciation which must be made not once but many times – for courage is will power."[13]

Their officers set them an example. In 1814 an officer performed his duties within constant view of his subordinates, and although he suffered from the same fears and tensions as his men, he was expected to provide a model of behaviour under fire. A cool demeanour and the occasional quip such as that of the American officer who steadied his men ducking from shrapnel shells exploding overhead by admonishing them that "gentlemen bow only to ladies," went a long way to dispel the tension of combat.[14] There was no forgiveness for an officer who displayed signs of fear or lost control of his men in combat, as happened to one lieutenant at Chippawa. An officer's public display of courage, however, came at a high price – one British unit lost thirteen of seventeen officers engaged at Chippawa.

For generals, the size and congestion of the battlefield was a distinct advantage – they could see and maintain contact with their units and move quickly to any crucial spot. As the armies of the War of 1812 were relatively small, there was a high degree of centralization of command – orders could be quickly passed to subordinates and generals did not need large staffs. But generalship was a risky business in 1814 – of the six generals present at the battle of Lundy's Lane fought a few weeks after Chippawa, four were wounded, three severely. Because of his direct involvement in the battle, the small size of his staff, and his high degree of visibility, a general's mental and physical state during a battle was a matter of greater importance than it is today, where levels of command insulate him from his subordinates. In 1814, not only did a general have to be cool and collected, he had to *appear* cool and collected.

Of all the factors influential in the outcome of battle in 1814, however, the human factor was the most important. It was the steadfastness of the common soldier that decided the outcome, and when two opposing armies were matched in generalship, weapons, training, and tactics, victory would go to the side most determined to achieve it. The army possessing the attitude of "what we go for, we get, and what we get, we hold," the hallmark of high morale, often prevailed.[15] At Chippawa, both opponents possessed exactly that spirit.

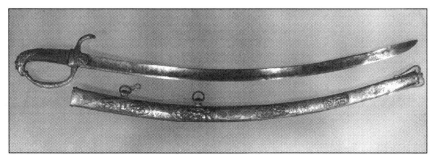

U.S. Artillery Officer's Sword, 1814
This ornate brass-hilted sabre, with an eagle's head pommel, was manufactured
in France for senior officers of the U.S. Artillery. Like their British counterparts,
American officers rarely had an opportunity to use these weapons in combat.
Courtesy West Point Museum, U.S. Military Academy

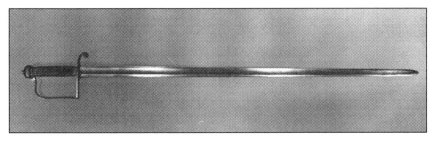

U.S. Infantry Sergeant's Sword, 1814
The sword was one of the badges of office of an infantry sergeant during the
War of 1812. In combat, however, he was more likely to use a musket than any
other weapon.
Courtesy West Point Museum, U.S. Military Academy

U.S. Infantry Platoon, War of 1812
Although Scott's First Brigade wore the famous grey jacket, the regular infantry of Ripley's Second Brigade were issued with the dark blue coatee. This modern painting shows a platoon (in 1814 an *ad hoc* unit for fire and manoeuvre organized before battle) of American infantry formed in a two-rank line. Behind the two firing ranks can be seen the rank of "file closers" composed of sergeants and junior officers whose job it was to adjust the firing ranks when casualties were taken.
Painting by H.C. McBarron, courtesy Parks Canada

U.S. Infantryman, 1813-1814, Service Dress
This private soldier, wearing the blue uniform, is biting off a cartridge prior to loading his Springfield musket. For comfort, he has pushed his cartridge box, or cartouche, behind his back, while over his white cross belts can be seen the straps for the knapsack on his back. The belts of his canteen and cloth haversack, containing his rations, hang on his left hip. The regular infantry of both armies dressed for display rather than utility.
Painting by H.C. McBarron, courtesy Parks Canada

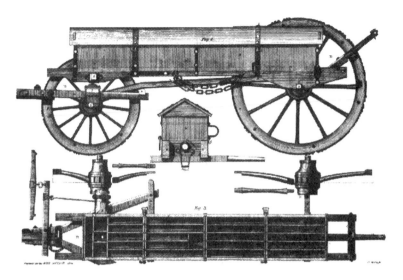

U.S. Artillery Caisson, 1814

An ammunition caisson of the type based on a French pattern probably used by Hindman's battalion at the battle of Chippawa. Although the ammunition chest was removable, it was usually left in place in action and was a vulnerable target. During the battle, one British artillery caisson exploded from an American shell.

From Henri Othon De Scheel, *Treatise of Artillery*, Philadelphia, 1800, reprinted by Museum Restoration Service, Bloomfield, 1984. Courtesy Museum Restoration Service

Plan of an American Iron Field Howitzer of the War of 1812

Unlike field guns, which fired solid round shot, howitzers fired explosive shells and were useful, if somewhat erratic, weapons that were included in the field artillery of most nations during the Napoleonic period. Both the British and American artillery at Chippawa brought 5.5 inch howitzers into action.

From Louis de Tousard, *American Artillerist's Companion*, Philadelphia, 1809

British Brass Field Gun, 1813
This 9-pdr. gun is mounted on a block trail carriage and is complete with its implements and side-arms; note the muzzle tompion, ready-use ammunition chests on either side of the barrel, and buckets.
Photo by D.R. Hough, courtesy Museum Restoration Service, Bloomfield, Canada

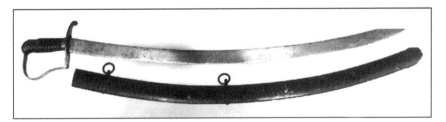

U.S. Light Dragoon Sabre, War of 1812
This Model 1813 Light Dragoon Sabre manufactured by Nathan Starr was carried by Captain Samuel D. Harris's cavalrymen at the battle. They found no opportunity to use it.
Courtesy West Point Museum, U.S. Military Academy

British Brass 12-pdr. Field Gun, War of 1812
This picture shows the construction of the sturdy block-trail carriages used by British artillery at Chippawa. Although sizable, field guns presented a small frontage and were difficult targets for opposing artillery. It was more common to neutralize artillery by killing the gun detachments and horse teams.
Courtesy Museum Restoration Service, Bloomfield, Canada

Soldier, 19th Light Dragoons, British Army, Full Dress
The 19th Light Dragoons' uniform was not particularly well suited for service in the rough terrain of North America. Nor did they find many opportunities to engage in the British cavalryman's favourite tactic – the charge.
Painting by C.W. Jefferys, courtesy National Archives of Canada, C-128839

U.S. Model 1808 Infantry Cartridge Box
The wooden block inserted into the box contained 38 holes for cartridges while a flap opening on the front gave access to a storage compartment for cleaning materials for the musket. British infantry carried a similar piece of equipment, but as the regulations of both armies at Chippawa stated that the men must carry 60 rounds, the blocks may have been removed and cartridges crammed into the pouch itself.
Courtesy Frederick C. Gaede collection

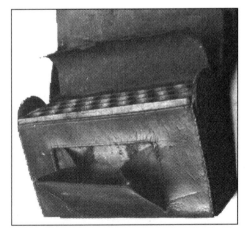

U.S. Model 1795 Musket, .69 Calibre
Commonly called the "Springfield musket," this was the standard long arm of American infantry during the war and derived from a French weapon supplied during the revolutionary war. During the War of 1812, contracts were let out to private manufacturers such as Eli Whitney who manufactured this particular weapon in 1812. American weapons production was impressive. It is estimated that by 1814 about thirty thousand muskets were being produced annually in the United States.
Courtesy Parks Canada

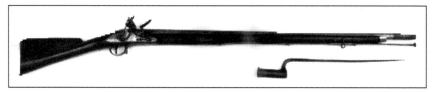

British India Pattern Musket, .75 Calibre
The standard infantry musket of British infantry during the war, the India Pattern was a cheaper and more easily manufactured version of the Short Land Pattern Musket. It fired a one ounce ball that, at close range, could penetrate five inches of oak and break large limb bones.
Courtesy Parks Canada

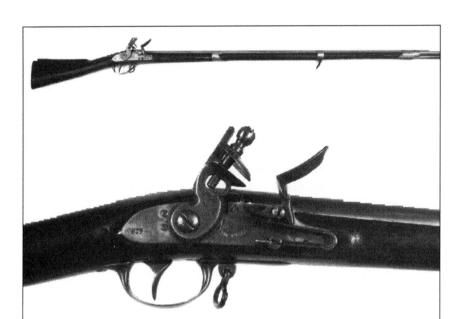

U.S. Model 1795 Musket, .69 Calibre

This particular weapon was manufactured at the government armoury at Springfield in 1809. Firing a lighter and smaller ball than its British counterpart, the Springfield had less hitting power. The enlargement shows details of the ignition system. The screw clamp jaws of the cock held a flint that, when the trigger was pulled, was brought into contact with the frizzen, a hinged piece of steel (here shown in the open position), striking sparks that ignited the powder in the pan (between the cock and the frizzen) that set off the charge in the barrel by means of the vent hole (not shown).

Courtesy Parks Canada

Private, Glengarry Light Infantry
Fencibles, 1814
In contrast to the line infantry who
were trained to fight in compact
formations, each British infantry
regiment had one company of light
infantry who fought in a looser
formation and who were used as
advance and rear guards. The army
in North America also possessed an
entire regiment of this type, the
Glengarry Light Infantry, recruited
in eastern Upper Canada. The
Glengarries wore a dark green uniform that earned them the nickname
of the "black stumps."
Painting by G.A. Embleton, courtesy Parks Canada

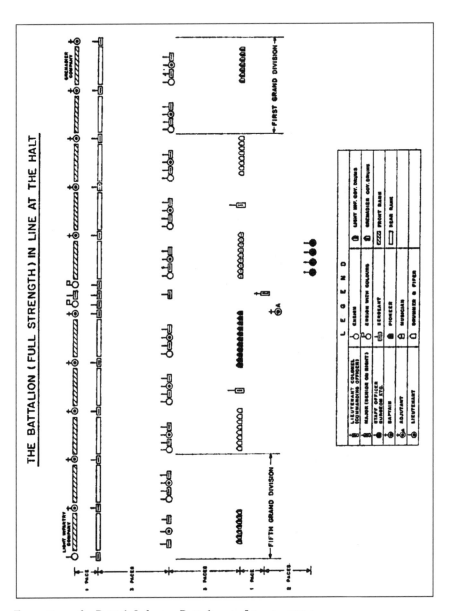

Formation of a British Infantry Battalion in Line in 1814
This schematic shows a British infantry battalion of ten companies drawn up in a line of two ranks. Note the positions of the grenadier and light infantry companies on the flanks and the colour party in the center of the front rank. Three paces (a pace is 2 1/2 feet) behind the rear rank is the rank of "file closers," junior officers and sergeants, whose task it is to align the two front ranks as casualties are taken. At Chippawa on 5 July 1814, the 1st and 100th Foot advanced in this formation toward Winfield Scott's waiting First Brigade.
Courtesy *Canadian Geographic Magazine*

CHAPTER 5

"AN EXCITEMENT AMONG
THE PEOPLE"
The Invasion of Canada, 3 - 4 July 1814

Brown's orders for the invasion of Canada were read out to the Left Division at the evening roll call on 2 July 1814. During the day, accompanied by Scott, Porter and his two engineer officers, Lieutenant Colonel William McRee and Major Eleazar D. Wood, the American commander had reconnoitred the Canadian shore of the river and devised a plan for the landing operation. Scott's First Brigade was to cross in small boats from Black Rock and land near the ferry station on the Canadian shore north of Fort Erie. Owing to a lack of transport, part of Brigadier General Eleazar Ripley's Second Brigade would cross with Scott, while the remainder, in whatever craft were available and three small United States Navy schooners, were to land at Snake Hill below the fort. The two brigades would then encircle the fort, and Brown calculated that by daylight he would have brought across his heavy artillery and could begin battering the British post into submission.[1]

As the troops moved to their embarkation points around midnight on 2 July, it began to rain. There was some confusion at the embarkation points, but by about 2 a.m. Scott rowed for the Canadian side. Visibility was obscured both by darkness and rain and mist. As the leading craft neared the Canadian shore, they were spotted by the picket of an officer and twenty men of the 100th Foot posted at the ferry station for just such an occurrence. They opened a "galling" fire that became more accurate as the range decreased.[2]

Wanting to inspire his men, Scott decided to get to grips with the enemy as soon as possible. He tested the water with his sword, and finding it only knee deep, plunged in. He was about to give the command, "follow me!" when he sank up to his neck and was only able to blurt out, "too deep!" Forced to swim for his life and encumbered by his cloak, hat, and boots, Scott was "in jeopardy from fire and water" until the boat came round and hauled the thoroughly soaked general to safety. Given the tall Virginian's reputation as a disciplinarian, probably no one in the craft laughed outright at Scott's bedraggled figure – but there must have been more than a few stifled grins.[3]

As the boats grounded on the west bank of the river, the British picket fell back into darkness. The landing below the fort went fairly smoothly, and by the time Brown crossed the river at dawn the First Brigade with units of the Second Brigade were formed ready to move against the British post. Ripley's Second Brigade had a more difficult time above the fort, because of a shortage of transport and the mist and fog on the lake. It was not until 6 a.m. that his men were ashore. One member of the division was totally oblivious to what was going on around him. The strenuous activities of the previous hours had been too much for an exhausted Jarvis Hanks, the fourteen-year-old drummer boy of the Eleventh Infantry. He fell fast asleep on his feet as his unit waited for orders.[4]

After the rainfall in the night, the division was glad that Sunday, 3 July 1814, dawned clear and warm. Brown ordered Scott to send Major Thomas Jesup's Twenty-Fifth Infantry closer to Fort Erie to "observe the movements of the garrison as they might blow up the works and attempt an escape." At the same time, he directed his adjutant-general, Colonel Charles K. Gardner, to take that part of Ripley's brigade that had landed with Scott and envelop the fort. Accompanied by his staff, Brown then went forward to reconnoitre. This being a Sunday, he encountered a local "inhabitant and his son (a small boy) on their way to the river to fish" and by "threats and promises," secured the services of this man as a guide.[5]

When the Twenty-Fifth closed on the fort, they came under sporadic artillery fire that wounded four of Jesup's men. The men in the ranks fully expected that they would have to attack the British post "and carry it by storm as it was supposed to be well manned and fortified."[6] While his engineer officers sited gun positions, Brown gave orders for the artillery to be brought across as soon as possible. The first pieces, some 18-pdr. guns, were being wheeled into position that early afternoon when a British officer emerged from the fort with an offer of surrender.[7]

The British commandant of Fort Erie, Major Thomas Buck of the 8th Foot, had been in a dilemma all day. His orders from Major General Phineas Riall assured him that his post, having "been placed in that state of defence which it is conceived affords perfect security to its Garrison" would be able "to resist an attack short of an Invasion in force."[8] As he gazed at the hundreds of American troops manoeuvring around his post, it was clear to Buck that an "invasion in force" was exactly what he faced.

The British officer had little confidence that his small stone fort, armed with three artillery pieces and garrisoned by a company of infantry with a detachment of gunners, would be able to resist such strength for long. Described as "a mild, honorable, and pleasant man, rather small, but good looking," the thirty-five-year-old Buck talked it over with his officers. Most advised him to surrender "from motives of humanity" in order to avoid "a useless sacrifice of men's lives," but not all were in agreement. Lieutenant Joseph Maxwell of the 100th Foot wanted to fight to the death, and many of the infantry, veterans of Captain Thomas Dawson's company of the same regiment who had been prominent in the attack on Fort Niagara the previous December, called out to the officers to defend the fort "to the last extremity."[9]

Nonetheless, Buck decided to surrender and midway through the afternoon sent out a flag of truce. The formalities took about two hours to complete, but about 5 p.m. the British garrison of 137 officers and men marched out "under the Tune of Yonca Doodle" (as that atrocious speller Captain Benjamin Ropes recorded) played by American fifes and drums, and crossed to captivity in the United States.[10] A few minutes later they were replaced by a company of U.S. artillery and a new flag flew over Fort Erie.[11]

One part of Buck's command that escaped captivity was the small detachment of the 19th Light Dragoons posted at the fort. As soon as word of the American crossing had reached him the night before, Buck had dispatched them to warn Riall. The British commander received news of the invasion at his headquarters at Fort George at about 8 a.m. and quickly issued his orders. Five companies of the 1st Foot were moved forward from Fort George to Chippawa to reinforce the garrison at that place while the remainder of the division was alerted, as were the local militia units and the various groups of native warriors. Riall then rode south to Chippawa with his staff.[12]

The alarm was sounded throughout the Canadian side of the Niagara that pleasant summer Sunday. Captain W. Hamilton Merritt of the Niagara Light Dragoons was taking a well-deserved leave at his family's home at the Twelve-Mile Creek near Lake Ontario. It being Merritt's twenty-first birthday, he had invited a number of friends to dinner, but when they did not show up, he sat down with his family to enjoy the repast. A dragoon suddenly "arrived with the news of the enemy having landed" and, in a few minutes, the young militia officer was riding hard for Fort George.[13]

In later years, Private George Ferguson of the 100th Foot remembered that particular Sabbath well. A devout Methodist lay preacher, Ferguson had obtained permission from his commanding officer to leave Fort George in order to preach at Christian Warner's chapel in Stamford, between Queenston and Chippawa. He was in the midst of his sermon when

> there was quite an excitement among the people and some were calling aloud for mercy, there came an express for a Militia officer who was in the congregation that the American Army had crossed at Black Rock. This threw the Congregation into confusion – the people ran to secure their effects – one running here and another there. I felt calm and tranquil, and my trust was in the Lord Jehovah.[14]

Word of the invasion reached Captain John Norton near the falls of Niagara, where he was encamped with about three hundred western and Grand River warriors. On Riall's orders, Norton had been preparing a reconnaissance of the American side of the Niagara. Now, he was summoned to Chippawa with his men by Lieutenant Colonel Thomas Pearson, the commanding officer at that place.

Arriving after a quick march, Norton and his warriors joined Pearson in a reconnaissance toward Fort Erie. Moving cautiously south down the river road, they encountered no Americans until they reached a point near the ferry station where they found the enemy "in strong force." Rumours were rampant, and local inhabitants told Pearson that another American force had landed at Point Abino on Lake Erie and was proceeding to Chippawa by a back road, while still another body intended to cross that day near the Grand Island. The veteran Pearson was not panicked by these reports, but realizing that he could do little with the small force under his command (which consisted of only Norton's warriors and the two flank companies of the 100th Foot), he posted pickets on the river road and withdrew to Chippawa during the evening.[15]

There he found Riall, who had arrived from Fort George with the five companies of the 1st Foot, most of the squadron of 19th Light Dragoons, and Captain James Mackonochie's mobile field brigade (battery) of artillery. The 1st and 2nd Lincoln Militia were ordered to march for Chippawa as was the 8th Foot, Riall's third regular battalion, on its way from York.

Chippawa was a strong position. The southernmost terminus of the Canadian portage route around the falls, it had been an established military post since 1791. Since that time, a small community, uncharitably described in 1810 as "a mean village of twenty houses, three stores, two taverns, a windmill and a distillery," had grown up around the garrison.[16] The village was divided by the Chippawa River, a "dull, muddy river running through flat, swampy country," which at its junction with the Niagara River, was about 250 feet wide and crossed by a high, narrow, rickety wooden bridge.[17] On the north bank, sited to cover the bridge, was a line of entrenchments and a redoubt constructed the previous spring by the 8th Foot. The river was fordable further upstream, but the country to the west was also swampy and obstructed, presenting an obstacle to the movement of large bodies of troops. Impossible to flank on the east because of the Niagara River, difficult to flank on the west, and hard to attack in front, Chippawa offered Riall the best defensive position on the Canadian side of the Niagara River.[18]

Unaware that the garrison of Fort Erie had surrendered, the British commander wanted to attack while the Americans were pre-occupied in besieging that post, and while they were still getting their heavy equipment across the river. But, as he only had two regular battalions, he decided to postpone an advance until the 8th Foot, expected momentarily, arrived. As the sun set on 3 July, Riall and his men settled down to wait for events.[19]

In the Left Division's camp near the ferry station, the morning of 4 July dawned sunny and bright. During the morning, all units fired a general salute in honour of the national holiday. If there were any in the ranks who still expected to get time off for the traditional 4th of July dinner, they were sadly mistaken. Late in the morning, Brown ordered Scott to take his brigade, two companies of artillery, and Captain Samuel Harris's troop of light dragoons north to the Chippawa River. Scott was "to be governed by circumstances," but was to take "care to secure a good military position for the night."[20]

The First Brigade set off about noontime. Brown planned to follow as soon as possible with the remainder of the division, but not until late in the day did his boatmen, who had been working tirelessly for nearly thirty-six hours, finish transporting the division's artillery, baggage, supplies, and wagons – not to mention 450 horses (the grain-fuelled prime movers of the time) from the American side. It was nearly 4 p.m. before the remainder of the division set out for Chippawa.[21]

Scott, meanwhile, made good progress north on the river road. Then as now, it was a pleasant journey along the cool banks of the Niagara on a straight road shaded by tall, leafy trees. The comfortable atmosphere of the march was dispelled, however, when the brigade approached Frenchman's Creek, four miles north of Fort Erie. Harris's dragoons, who were in the advance, rode back with news that a British force was in position on the far side of the stream.

These troops were commanded by Pearson who had received information about the American advance from the pickets he had posted the previous day on the river road. With Riall's agreement, he had assembled a select force and marched south hoping to delay the enemy. Pearson's command consisted of both flank companies of the 100th Foot, the light company of the 1st Foot, Lieutenant Richard S. Armstrong's two 24-pdr. guns, and a strong detachment of the 19th Light Dragoons under Lieutenant William Horton.

Thomas Pearson was an experienced light infantry officer with nearly twenty years service who had seen action in Holland, Egypt, Denmark, and the West Indies before serving with Wellington in Spain. His thigh bone shattered at the battle of Albuera in 1811, he had been posted to a less demanding position in Canada as an inspecting field officer of militia, only to find himself in the middle of a hot war. The constant pain he suffered from his wound left him with an irritable disposition, and he tended to be impatient with the military pretensions of Canadian militia officers. They detested him, but Pearson could not have cared less.

The veteran was in his element on this fine summer day. The recent heavy rain had flooded Frenchman's Creek and it was not fordable near its junction with the Niagara. Pearson ordered his men to tear up the floor planks of the bridge and then posted his infantry and two guns to cover the approaches to the bridge. Meanwhile Horton's dragoons took station upstream to prevent any attempt to cross the creek and outflank the British position.

Coming up to the ruined bridge, Scott was forced to deploy from column of march into battle formation and to unlimber his guns to prepare for attack. Before anything got going, however, Armstrong saluted the Americans with a round from one of his two 24-pdrs. Pearson's infantry added a complementary volley, and the British then disappeared up the river road covered by Horton's dragoons. It was fortunate for Scott that the British had not had time to burn or destroy the bridge planking, but he was still delayed while he awaited repairs to the bridge. The First Brigade got underway again but, three miles to the north at Winterhoot's (now Miller's) Creek, they again found Pearson behind a creek. And so it went, creek after creek, for nearly fourteen long, hot, dusty miles as the veteran officer did a superb job of delaying the American advance.[22]

By the late afternoon, the lead American elements had reached Street's (now Ussher's) Creek, the last stream before Chippawa. North of this was a flat, open area of farm fields extending some distance back from the river. Captain Turner Crooker of the Ninth Infantry, whose company formed the left flank guard of Scott's column, emerged from the woods upstream of the bridge. Seeing a chance to cut off the retreat of two British guns, Crooker ordered his men to cross the chest-deep stream. They emerged in an open area north of the creek.

In his excitement, Crooker had forgotten about the British dragoons. Horton, on the other hand, was vigilant and spotted the small American unit crossing the open field – unsupported by any other troops. Seeing fair game, he ordered a charge.

Before the horrified eyes of the First Brigade who could see Crooker's plight but could not assist him, the blue-uniformed British dragoons swept across the farm field toward the little knot of grey-clad Americans. Keeping his head, Crooker ordered his men to fire one volley at the horsemen and then head for a nearby farmhouse. From this shelter, they knocked down eight horses and wounded four dragoons, bringing Horton's dreams of cavalry glory to a close. It was a neatly-fought little action and Scott later reported that he had "witnessed nothing more gallant in partizan war than ... the conduct of Captain Crooker and his company."[23] Horton's charge, however, had allowed Armstrong to get his guns safely across the Chippawa.[24]

Norton and his warriors now arrived on the scene. On 4 July the previous day, they had returned to their camp near the falls and it was not until 2 p.m. that they were ordered back to Chippawa. Although Norton moved as quickly as possible, he did not reach the village until after Pearson had marched out. Moving south, the warriors soon heard "firing in our front" and then met Pearson's men north of Street's Creek. "Supposing the Americans to be in rear," Norton "hastened forward with those near me, but our Rear was influenced by the retrograde movement, and did not follow us." The warriors "remained in flank, till the Troops had passed, and then retired." As the last man crossed the bridge over the Chippawa River to safety, British engineers dropped the centre section of the rickety structure into the river.[25]

It was nearly dusk when Scott's column approached Chippawa. The village was shrouded in smoke from burning houses on the south bank of the river, which Riall had ordered set on fire to deny the enemy any cover close to the bridge. As the American column came within range, the British guns on the north bank took them under fire. It was obvious to Scott that there was no chance of seizing the bridge by surprise, and as his men were thirsty and tired after almost six hours of constant skirmishing he decided to carry out his orders and find "a good military position for the night." Turning the brigade in its tracks, he withdrew under a heavy downpour of rain two miles to a possible camp site he had noted south of Street's creek.[26]

Near midnight Brown arrived with Ripley's Second Brigade, and the division's artillery and train. Having marched nearly fifteen miles under continuous thunderstorms and rain, they were cold, wet, and tired, and glad to fall out of the ranks and get some rest. As that atrocious speller, Captain Benjamin Ropes, recalled:

> ... after Detailing, posting guards we ha[d] Liberty to lie down on the ground for two or three hours which was covered with water owing to the Clayey surfise, this was the first rist that I had received from the Night of the first Inst. & it was very switt although wit & Lying as it ware on water.[27]

View of Niagara Falls from the Canadian Bank, 1805
The battle of Chippawa was fought about three miles south of the falls of Niagara, depicted in this 1805 watercolour. The houses in the foreground are in the little hamlet of Bridgewater Mills, which was burned to the ground by the Left Division on 26 July 1814.
Watercolour by George Heriot, courtesy National Archives of Canada, C-12797

The Niagara River from the Mouth of Street's (Ussher's) Creek
This is a view looking south up the river. On the right is the mouth of the creek, on the left Navy Island. The Niagara formed a convenient logistical route for the Left Division, and throughout July 1814 their supplies moved by boat from Buffalo to a terminus point at Samuel Street's farm.
Photograph by Robert Foley, 5 July 1993

The Left Division Crosses the Niagara, 2-3 July 1814
This dramatic, if inaccurate, woodcut shows Scott watching as his First Brigade embarks in boats for the Canadian bank shown in the background. Actually the First Brigade crossed in darkness, and the artillery did not cross until the following afternoon.
From David Strother, *An Illustrated Life of General Winfield Scott*, New York, 1847

North East Demi-Bastion and Main Gate, Fort Erie
Although Riall hoped that the small garrison of Fort Erie would hold out long
enough to delay the American advance, the commandant, Major Thomas Buck
of the 8th Foot, opted to surrender "from motives of humanity" during the afternoon of 3 July 1814.
Photograph by Paul Kelly, courtesy *Canadian Military History* journal

Vedette, 19th Light Dragoons
Throughout the day of 4 July 1814, Scott's advance north to the Chippawa was
delayed by a British force under Lieutenant Colonel Thomas Pearson that
included a troop of the 19th Light Dragoons commanded by Lieutenant
William Horton. Just north of Street's Creek, Horton caught a company of the
Ninth U.S. Infantry isolated in a field and charged to cut them down.
Drawing by A. Robinson-Sager, courtesy Parks Canada

Country Lane Near the Niagara River

The Canadian side of the Niagara was in an advanced state of settlement by 1814. The river road along which the Left Division advanced north to the Chippawa was intersected by country lanes like this bordered by split-rail fences. Similar fences cut across the battlefield at Chippawa.

Watercolour by Sir James Estcourt, 1838, courtesy National Archives of Canada, C-93975

War Chief, Grand River Nations
Pro-British native warriors fought hard at Chippawa and suffered heavy casualties. This war chief wears the usual mix of European and native dress and, as a sign of his rank, an engraved gorget or neck piece presented to him by the Crown.
Painting by G.A. Embleton, courtesy Parks Canada

CHAPTER 6

"WE HAD CONSIDERABLE SCIRMUSHING THE FOORNOON"
The Morning of 5 July 1814

The camp site selected by Scott lay in the triangle of land formed by Street's Creek and the Niagara. Brown thought it a good position, with its "right resting on the river and a ravine [Street's Creek] in front."[1] Others were not so generous. Writing after the war, Major General James Wilkinson criticized a site that "possessed no attribute of a judicious position *offensive or defensive*" as it was "formed in a narrow fork, made by the river and a deep miry creek" and "was liable to be turned on the left and attacked in rear."[2]

To secure the perimeter of the camp, pickets were posted on the most likely avenues of approach, while the field pieces of Captains Thomas Biddle, Nathan Towson, and John Ritchie were placed in defensive positions. Towson's company was on the north face of the camp near the bridge over the creek; Ritchie's company was in the northwest angle and Biddle's the southwest angle of the camp. For greater security, Towson's guns were emplaced behind an earthwork, and the other two companies may have done the same. The guns of the artillery reserve rested along the length of the river road that formed the eastern face of the camp.[3]

The American camp was part of an extensive clearing on the bank of the Niagara river "embellished with fine farms."[4] Most of the camp lay on the land of Samuel Street. A native of Connecticut, Street had come to the Niagara area during the Revolutionary war to sell supplies to the British army. Since that time, he had had a varied career as merchant and land speculator, and had also served as judge of the district court and deputy paymaster of the militia of Upper Canada. Prominent in local affairs, Street had been elected several times to the provincial legislative assembly and had served twice as its Speaker.

In the 1790s, Street had acquired a large property along the Niagara River that included the land between Chippawa River and the creek named after him, as well as property on the south side of that creek. With the assistance of his daughter, Mary, and her husband, John Ussher, Street had worked hard to make this large holding, known variously as the "Grove" or "Pine Grove Farm," a prosperous concern.

There were at least two houses on the farm. Although evidence is somewhat sketchy, Street occupied a large frame building, possibly located south of the creek. North of the creek there was a smaller house in which John and Mary Ussher lived, a barn, a stable, and a storehouse with an adjoining wharf near the Niagara River.

According to his subsequent claims for wartime losses, Samuel Street engaged in mixed farming. The Grove possessed a herd of dairy and beef cattle, five hogs, and fifteen shoats; there were tons of hay in the barn, and the fields were ripe with a crop of oats and peas. But when the Americans arrived late on 4 July, they found Pine Grove farm deserted. On Riall's orders, Mary Ussher had driven most of the cattle over the Chippawa bridge that afternoon, leaving the pigs, two dairy cows and their calves, and one riding mare at the farm. Not surprisingly, these animals disappeared into the service of the United States.[5]

The most notable feature of the Grove Farm was the large area of cleared fields north of Street's Creek. Called the "plain" in many accounts of the battle (and a term that will be used below), it was about five to seven hundred yards wide near the mouth of Street's Creek and extended north toward Chippawa, where one participant remembered it as being about "a third narrower."[6] Most of the farm buildings were located on this plain close to the river road, and the plain itself appears to have been bounded on all sides by split-rail fences. Drummer Jarvis Hanks recalled that the area was covered by "grass about three feet high and very thrifty"[7] – possibly he was talking about Samuel Street's oat field.

The course of Street's Creek was demarcated by a "range of thick bushes."[8] These bushes were so dense that, to one witness, the course of the creek appeared to be "a bank about five feet high in a straight line."[9] Due to the recent heavy rainfall, the creek was high, and it was described as being chest deep and impassable to wagons and gun carriages.[10]

Surrounding the farm were dense pine woods interspersed with clearings. These woods were poorly drained and obstructed by fallen trees, as they had been logged frequently. Between the plain and the Chippawa River, these pine woods connected to a strip of woodland which had never been cleared, some quarter of a mile in breadth, extending from the forest to within some 10 to 15 rods [165 to 247 1/2 feet] of the Niagara, and leaving between it and the bank of the river an open avenue, through which passed the great public highway [the river road], thus forming a masque between Chippawa and Street's Creek.[11]

During the wet night of 4-5 July, Captain Joseph Henderson's picket of the Twenty-Second Infantry, posted north of Street's Creek, watched this strip of woods. Toward morning, the rain finally began to tail off, and as the sky grew light shots rang out from the woods around the American position. Henderson's picket came under fire from snipers, who had crept along the bank of the Niagara River. He lost several wounded and Henderson himself was narrowly missed by a musket ball that "entered the knapsack upon which I was seated and then entered the sapling against which I was leaning close to my head."[12]

Henderson was relieved at 8 a.m. by Captain Benjamin Ropes's company of the Twenty-First Infantry. The forty-two-year-old Massachusetts native was not at all happy with this assignment, as he had "bin on Duty three Nights & two days & was afrid I should not be able to do my Duty." Still he obeyed his orders. Taking over, he reconnoitred his position, and concluding that standing sentries would only make good targets, instituted small patrols that constantly moved over the plain and river road north of the picket. Ropes placed his men in Ussher's barn, and ordering the north side of the building torn down used the lumber to construct a small breastwork across the river road to the Niagara River. These were wise precautions as British harassment continued throughout the morning, and in Ropes's words "we had considerable Scirmushing [in] the foornoon."[13]

At about the same time, Captain Joseph Treat's picket of the Twenty-First Infantry, located some distance from the southwest angle of the camp, came under severe fire that wounded several men. The picket fell back in confusion, leaving one of their wounded on the ground. Racing after his men, Treat was forced to leave the man momentarily while he tried to rally his company. This exchange of musketry attracted the attention of Captain Biddle's artillery company nearby. Ordering his gunners to fire canister into the woods to disperse the enemy, the twenty-four-year-old Biddle, the scion of a prominent Philadelphia family, mounted his horse and galloped to the scene. Placing the wounded man on his horse, he carried him to safety before helping Treat get control of his men.[14]

Unfortunately for Treat, this incident attracted the attention of Brown, who summarily decided that the captain had abandoned his wounded. The American commander's justice was quick and severe – within hours, he issued a general order stating that "Capt. Treat shall no longer serve in the 21st Regt., nor in this division during the Campaign."[15]

Once started, the firing continued in a desultory fashion throughout the morning. Shooting from the cover of the woods and changing position immediately after each shot, the snipers were hard to spot. Their fire was largely inaccurate, but some casualties were taken. Brown was annoyed by the harassment, but having "no desire to show his own force" allowed the British to "indulge" themselves.[16]

Riall had not planned an attack on the American camp. The previous night he had ordered Norton to take a small party of warriors and "observe exactly the position of the Enemy, without giving any alarm by firing at the advanced posts, – & to return and give information of the same." Other parties, however, were dispatched on the same mission and, in Norton's words, "instead of a reconnoitring party it became a Band of Skirmishers, who began with firing at the Sentries, whom the Enemy having succoured, compelled them to retire."[17]

Riall received constant information from these parties, which consisted of "Militia Men of good character, and intelligence, and of Indians who got close to them [the Americans], and climbed Trees to overlook their Position."[18] Still unaware that Fort Erie had fallen, he was convinced that much of the American division was at that place and, at most, he faced a force of about two thousand men.

His own strength was augmented during the morning by the arrival of the 8th Foot and the 1st and 2nd Lincoln Regiments of the Canadian militia. Concerned about the security of his rear, however, Riall immediately ordered the 1st Lincolns, "the best skirmishers in the country," back to Queenston.[19] He then took stock of his situation.

The British general now had a sizable force under command comprising nearly 1400 regular infantry, 200 militia of the 2nd Lincoln Regiment, 300 native warriors, Major Robert Lisle's squadron of the 19th Light Dragoons, and Mackonochie's artillery brigade. The decision facing him was whether to remain on the defensive in his entrenchments on the north bank of the Chippawa, or to cross the river and attack.[20]

Not entirely convinced of the accuracy of the information he was receiving, Riall reconnoitred the American camp late in the morning with Norton and Pearson. He must have liked what he saw, as around noon, according to Norton, the British commander decided to attack as soon as his engineers repaired the bridge over the Chippawa so that his artillery could pass to the opposite bank.[21]

The village was soon full of military bustle as Riall's men made ready. The infantry checked flint and priming, and carefully loaded a round into their muskets. Their officers made sure that each man had sixty rounds of ball cartridge, while the regimental quartermasters stocked the reserve ammunition in small, sturdy two-wheeled carts that remained safely to the rear of the battalion. Mackonochie's gunners undertook last minute repairs to their harness, gun carriages and caissons, and fed and watered the gun team horses. The troopers of the 19th Light Dragoons tended to their mounts in a similar fashion and looked to the edge of their sabres. Occasionally, over the noise of marching columns, the rumble of artillery carriages, the firing of test shots, and the shouting of orders, the sound of hammering could be heard from the bridge as Riall's engineers worked to restore the centre section of the rickety structure. They were sweating as the day had become quite hot.

Newcomers marched into this busy scene. Captain John Rowe's company of the 2nd Lincolns had assembled the previous day at Queenston with the other companies of the regiment, and arrived at Chippawa as a unit that morning. The men of the company may have grumbled about the logic of the military mind, as many of them lived not far from Chippawa, and probably saw no good reason why they had to march seven miles north on Monday and ten miles south on Tuesday just to please some "Britisher" officer.[22]

Rowe's company, drawn from an area near the falls of Niagara, was typical of the sedentary militia under Riall's command, consisting mostly of farmers, of which many were family related. Rowe, a former sergeant of Butler's Rangers, had seen considerable service during the Revolutionary War. There were many former Americans in the company's ranks. Rowe's lieutenant, Christopher Buchner, was a New Jerseyman who had come to Canada soon after the Revolution to farm. He settled on the large sand hill that overlooked the junction of the portage road and a pleasant side route known locally as Lundy's Lane. His wife, Sarah, was the daughter of James Forsyth, another Loyalist, who farmed and owned a tavern midway between Buchner's place and Chippawa. Sarah's brother, also James Forsyth, was a private in Rowe's company. Another of Buchner's neighbours, Stephen Peer, resided with his wife, Lydia, in a neat white frame house below the hill. Peer was a recent immigrant from the United States who had married into the numerous Skinner clan, a Loyalist family who farmed south of Buchner's place. He may have been somewhat reluctant to march to Chippawa on 5 July, as his wife was eight months pregnant with their second child. Finally there was thirty-seven-year-old William Biggar, formerly of Bucks County, Pennsylvania. Now a tailor and farmer in Upper Canada, he had married the daughter of Charles Green, yet another Buchner neighbour.[23]

Also among the new arrivals was Private George Ferguson of the 100th Foot. Although he had no orders to do so, Ferguson had decided to rejoin his unit lest he be accused of desertion. He was only back with his company a few minutes when he was approached by one of his officers, Lieutenant George Williams, who "expressed his fears and apprehensions that he would fall in the field" and requested Ferguson to make sure that his trunks were sent to his wife. When Ferguson pointed out that he might also fall in action and advised the officer to place his possessions in the military store, Williams replied that he wished Ferguson to undertake this task as "I know you to be a man of God, and I can trust you, and Mrs. Williams considers you as such." The erstwhile preacher was highly pleased with this mark of respect.[24]

Private Ferguson's new commanding officer, Lieutenant Colonel George Hay, the Marquis of Tweeddale, was another new arrival at Chippawa that busy morning. A twice-wounded veteran of Wellington's army, the twenty-six-year-old Tweeddale had just caught up with his regiment. Almost as soon as he rode in, he was stricken by an attack of fever and forced to retire to bed, but had no sooner done so, than he was summoned to see Riall. Unable to rise, Tweeddale "returned the answer that I was in the cold fit of ague and I expected the hot fit in a short time," but would come when that passed. Riall considerately postponed the meeting for an hour.[25]

Brown had no idea of the British activities as the strip of woodland effectively blocked the Chippawa from American view. By midday, however, the American general had had enough of the incessant sniping. Word having reached him that Brigadier General Porter was approaching the camp, he rode south to meet the commander of the Third Brigade.

Porter had crossed over from the United States the previous night. His brigade was still not complete and he brought with him only his native warriors and Colonel James Fenton's Fifth Regiment of Pennsylvania Volunteers. The crossing had not been without incident. Some of Fenton's men took refuge in their constitutional rights and refused to serve outside the territorial United States – in disgust, he left them behind and crossed with the remainder. Lacking tents, the brigade had spent an uncomfortable night in the rain, and then without any breakfast commenced the long march to join the division. By noon, when Brown rode up with his staff, Porter's column had reached a point a few miles short of the camp.[26]

Brown informed Porter that

the position of the army (although doubtless) the best that could have been selected in that neighbourhood) proved to be a very troublesome and inconvenient one from its restricted limits, there being but three-fourths of a mile between the river and an almost impenetrable forest, which was swarming with Indians and militia, accustomed to its haunts ... and who were constantly firing upon and driving in his pickets ... and thereby exposing the whole camp to these troublesome visitants.[27]

Assuring the New Yorker that there was not a "single [regular] British soldier" on the south bank of the Chippawa, Brown ordered him to "scour the woods with [his] Indian force, sustained by the volunteers, and drive the enemy across" that river.[28]

View of Niagara Falls from the Table Rock
As British and Canadian troops moved south along the river road to assemble at
Chippawa on 4 and 5 July 1814, they may have caught a glimpse of the cataract
when they marched by this point.
Watercolour by Sempronius Stretton, courtesy National Archives of Canada, C-18824

Looking West Along Street's
(Ussher's) Creek, 1993
On the day of the battle, the
American camp was located south of
this creek. The thick bushes provided cover for British and Canadian
scouting parties that harassed the
Americans throughout the morning
of 5 July 1814. Flushed by recent
heavy rain, the creek was much
wider and deeper on the day of the
battle, one participant recalled it
being chest deep.
Photograph by Robert Foley, 5 July 1993

The South Bank of the Chippawa, 1986

Now part of a park, in 1814 this area was a cleared area of land divided from the battlefield by a strip of woodland that effectively hid the two armies from each other's observation. The present bridge over the Chippawa River is located considerably west of the 1814 bridge.

Author's photo

Sergeant, Royal Artillery, War of 1812

In every sense of the word an elite unit, the enlisted men of the Royal Artillery were better trained and paid than their infantry counterparts. They also had to be a minimum of 182 pounds, as this size was needed to manhandle the heavy equipment of the artillery.

Painting by Charles Stadden, courtesy Parks Canada

Captain, Royal Artillery, Full Dress Uniform, War of 1812

Unlike their infantry counterparts, the officers of the Royal Artillery and Royal Engineers were professionally educated at the Royal Military Academy at Woolwich before joining their respective corps. Throughout the war, the Royal Artillery made an important contribution to the fighting effectiveness of the British army.

Painting by Charles Stadden, courtesy Parks Canada

Chippawa Village and the King's Bridge in 1807
This watercolour looks east toward the Niagara River with the north bank of the
Chippawa River on the left. In July 1814, this bank was protected by fieldworks
with artillery in position. For Major General Phineas Riall, the Chippawa area
represented the best defensive position between Fort Erie and Lake Ontario.
Watercolour by George Heriot, courtesy National Archives of Canada, C-12768

The Chippawa River Looking West Upstream, 1838
The low banks of the river and the flat, swampy nature of the ground west of the
bridge made the village and bridge of Chippawa difficult to outflank to the west,
while the Niagara River made it impossible to outflank on the east. The bridge
over the Chippawa was thus a vitally important objective for both armies.
Watercolour by Sir James Estcourt, courtesy National Archives of Canada, C-93898

Street's Creek Bridge Looking South, 1860
On the morning of 5 July 1814, Winfield Scott's grey-uniformed First Brigade
crossed over this bridge while under fire from British artillery. To the right can
be seen the chimney of Samuel Street's residence, located south of the creek
near its bank.
From Benson Lossing, *Pictorial Field Book of the War of 1812*, New York, 1869

Street's Creek Bridge Looking North, 1860
The house and buildings in the background mark the right flank of Winfield
Scott's position near the house occupied by Samuel Street's daughter Mary and
her husband, John Ussher, in July 1814.
From Benson Lossing, *Pictorial Field Book of the War of 1812*, New York, 1869

CHAPTER 7

"SCENES OF INDESCRIBABLE HORROR": The Fight in the Woods

Porter's men were tired after their long march and he let them eat and get some rest before undertaking his attack. Thus, it was after 2 p.m. when he called for "volunteers to turn out and drive off the hostile Indians who had been firing on our pickets."[1] There was mixed response to this request. Captain Samuel White, from Gettysburg, Pennsylvania, recalled that "Fatigued as we were, having travelled ... about eighteen miles without rations, it is not to be wondered at, that not much alacrity was showed by the men to become of the party."[2]

Porter managed, however, to assemble a force of about two hundred Pennsylvanians and three hundred warriors. As a means of identification, he ordered the militiamen to leave their hats behind while the natives were instructed to tie a piece of white cloth around their heads. As the Pennsylvanians watched with fascination, the warriors, "many for the first time arrayed in the habiliments of battle costume," made ready.[3] Twenty-three-year-old Private Alexander McMullen from Franklin County looked on as one chief "in a speech, which for gesture and strength of lungs I had never heard equalled, was preparing them for their bloody deeds."[4] White remembered:

> The Indians tied up their heads with pieces of white muslin, ... which process must have consumed at least fifty yards ... they painted their faces, making red streaks above their eyes and foreheads – they then went to old logs and burnt stumps, and spitting upon their hands, rubbed them upon the burnt part, until they were perfectly black, when they drew their fingers down their cheeks leaving large black streaks – after this preparation they were ready for action or march.[5]

At about 3 p.m. Porter led his command in single file into the woods a half mile south of the camp. His numbers were bolstered by a detachment of fifty-six regular infantry under the command of Ripley's aide, Lieutenant William McDonald. When the warriors had disappeared into the trees, but the Pennsylvanians were still in the cleared fields near the Niagara, Porter halted and faced them to the right. His command now formed a continuous skirmish line, estimated as being between one-half and three quarters of a mile in length. On Porter's order, his men, preceded by scouts and followed by the regulars, moved north "with extreme caution and stillness."[6]

As they neared the area of thick brush near the upper reaches of Street's Creek, the scouts signalled the presence of the enemy. Porter passed orders to

> increase our speed as much as was consistent with the preservation of the order of the line, to receive the fire of the enemy, but not to return it until it could be done with certain effect, regardless of the fire of others; then to rush upon them with the warwhoop and to pursue, capture, and slaughter as many of them as practicable.[7]

Obeying, the Americans let the enemy fire first and then "rushed forward with savage yells." Outflanked by Porter's line, the British scouting parties had no choice but to pull out for Chippawa as fast as possible. Many were overrun, and in Porter's words, "scenes of indescribable horror" followed as a vicious fight took place with muskets, rifles, tomahawks, and scalping knives. Few of the British tried to surrender, most, "believing that no quarter was to be given, suffered themselves to be overtaken and cut down with the tomahawk, or turned upon their pursuers and fought to the last."[8]

The crackle of musketry and the howls and shrieks of the warriors of both sides could be clearly heard on the plain where Brown and his adjutant general, Colonel Charles Gardner, had ridden to watch the Third Brigade's progress. Brown had promised Porter the support of the First Brigade, but when the American commander had stopped at Scott's tent on his way through camp he was told that the tall fire-breather was sound asleep, and so Brown "thought [it] proper not to disturb him."[9]

Riding across the bridge of Street's Creek, Brown then came to Ropes's picket and ordered the Massachusetts native to have his patrols fire a few rounds and then fall back on the Usshers' house in an attempt to draw the British pickets forward. All this time, the "dreadful Yells" and scattered firing from the west continued as Porter's command drove the enemy steadily back to the Chippawa. Suddenly, Brown and Gardner became alert – the sounds of the fighting had changed – they could now make out disciplined volleys of musketry.[10]

As Porter's men chased the British through the pine woods, the more agile warriors had drawn ahead of the Pennsylvanians and regulars. Some distance to the rear, Porter was suddenly "surprised by a tremendous discharge of musketry," and a few minutes later his warriors came running back through the trees. With the help of their chiefs, Porter was able to check their flight and partially reform his line. Advancing "with caution to the margin of the wood" the Americans then "found themselves within a few yards of the British army drawn up in line of battle."[11]

The work of repairing the Chippawa bridge had taken longer than expected and it was after 3 p.m. before Riall ordered his troops over to the south bank. Once across, the regular infantry stayed in column of march on the road with Lisle's dragoons in advance. Under Pearson's command, the light companies of the 1st, 8th, and 100th Foot, and the 2nd Lincolns formed in the fields on the south bank of the river, supported by seventy western warriors. At his own request, Norton moved further to the right with about two hundred warriors in an attempt to outflank the enemy and attack the American camp from the rear. The troops could hear scattered firing gradually drawing closer. As they formed on the south bank, some of the British warriors who had survived the debacle in the woods, burst out of the tree line shouting "Yankee too strong! too many!"[12]

Pearson sent forward the Lincolns and the western warriors and they collided with Porter's natives coming full tilt in the opposite direction. A firefight ensued in the skirt of the woods, but the American braves got the worst of it and fell back. In a few minutes, however, rallied by their chiefs and Porter, they returned supported by Fenton's Pennsylvanians and McDonald's small detachment of regulars. A longer and more brutal struggle followed, and this time the Canadians and their native allies took heavy casualties.[13]

Porter remembered that "two or three vollies" were exchanged, while another commentator thought the skirmish lasted about fifteen minutes.[14] The result was disastrous for both the British warriors and Canadians. The natives lost one of their chiefs and hastily pulled back while the Lincolns' commanding officer, Lieutenant Colonel Thomas Dickson, a thirty-nine-year-old merchant from Queenston, was hit in the chest and knocked off his horse. Fortunately for Dickson, he had placed his glasses in his breast pocket and the direction of the musket ball "was turned by its striking my spectacles otherwise I must immediately have lost my life."[15] Four other

Lincoln officers went down, including Captain John Rowe. Lieutenant Christopher Buchner assumed command of Rowe's company, but it was sadly cut up. Among the dead were James Forsyth and Stephen Peer – the latter would never see his son, born twenty-six days later. The Lincolns began to waver, but they were rallied by fifty-five-year-old Major David Secord, a peacetime merchant from St. David's.[16]

Seeing their plight, Pearson detached the three regular light companies to their assistance, and it was their disciplined vollies that had alerted Brown and Gardner. Porter remembered that, after firing, the British "advanced impetuously upon us" and his men began to fall back in a most expeditious fashion. Unable to stop them, Porter gave the order to retreat and rally in the rear and then made his own exit.[17]

Another deadly race now took place as the British warriors and Canadian militia, followed by the light infantry, rushed forward hard on the heels of the fleeing Americans. Some of Norton's party took part in this chase, but without much success as their prey "outrun us, or eluded our Pursuit, from the intricate Nature of the Forest, impenetrable to the Sight for any distance."[18] It was a confused and bloody business, with small groups of frightened men stumbling into, and firing at each other, in the dense and obstructed terrain. Mistakes of identification were frequent and not a few men were shot by their comrades. Canadian militiaman John Wilson remembered:

> The moment we entered the woods we found ourselves sur-
> rounded by Indians. We supposed they were our own, but
> unfortunately for us they proved American, and two or
> three times our number. I was so near them that I asked
> which way they were going ... and not having a red coat
> the Indians evidently mistook me as much as I did them for
> they could not have missed me if they had directed a shot
> at me.[19]

Captain White of Fenton's regiment was not as fortunate. Seeing their men everywhere falling back, he and some fellow officers made their way to the split rail fence bordering the plain on the west, only to observe "British light horse advancing along the opposite side of the field at full speed." As there was no escape in that direction, White's party continued south along the fence and "concluded ourselves in perfect safety" when they were sud-denly surrounded by British warriors and put in the bag.[20]

Having disarmed the Americans, their captors' first enquiry was for money:

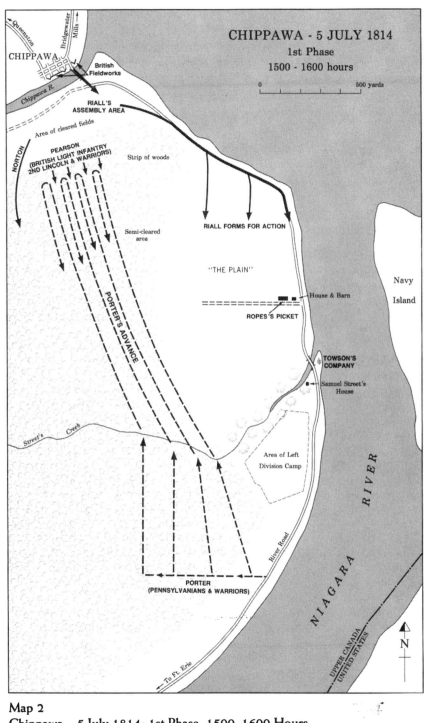

Map 2
Chippawa – 5 July 1814: 1st Phase, 1500–1600 Hours

A large Indian came up to me, calling out "money, money." – I insisted that I had none. He then seized my coat, which he took off me, another claimed my vest, another my neck-cloth, and so on, until they had stripped me of every article of cloathing, except my shirt and my pantaloons ... a fellow had placed his hand upon my watch chain, with a view to drawing it out of my pocket, but meeting with some little difficulty in consequence of my pocket being damp from perspiration, he deliberately drew his knife, when not wishing to give the gentleman the trouble of operating, I drew it out and handed it to him.[21]

Having dealt with first matters first, the warriors turned their prisoners about and began to dogtrot them back through the woods toward the Chippawa.

The survivors of Porter's force emerged from the woods near the American camp. Alexander McMullen, who had not gone out on the expedition because he did not have a weapon, was startled to see "the Indians and some of the volunteers flying across the fields toward us" having "received a warmer reception than they expected."[22] With the help of Captain Samuel Harris's dragoons, Porter halted the fugitives and began to reform them.[23]

In the meantime, Riall's regular troops moved south down the river road. Brown, still on the plain north of Ropes's picket, realized from "the cloud of dust rising and the heavy firing that the whole force of the enemy was in march and prepared for action."[24] He ordered Gardner to ride quickly to Scott with orders "to form his brigade ... and advance to 'meet the enemy'."[25]

Captain John Norton or the Snipe, Mohawk War Chief
The son of a Cherokee father and a Scottish mother, Norton was a resourceful, intelligent war chief who participated in almost every major battle of the Niagara campaigns of 1812, 1813, and 1814. After Tecumseh, he was the most successful British native leader of the war.
Oil portrait by Thomas Philips, R.A., c. 1818, Syon House, Brantford, U.K. Reproduced by gracious permission of the Duke of Northumberland

Grand River Mohawk Warrior
This warrior, painted in 1804, wears primarily native garb and has painted his face with red, black, and yellow pigments. During the afternoon of 5 July 1814, British and American warriors fought a bloody action in the woods to the west of Samuel Street's farm with no quarter given on either side.
Watercolour by Sempronius Stretton, courtesy National Archives of Canada, C-14827

Colonel Charles K. Gardner (1787-1869) in Later Life
Gardner was adjutant general of the Left Division and functioned as Brown's chief of staff and principal advisor. During the afternoon of 5 July 1814 he rode with Brown onto the plain north of the American camp to watch the results of Porter's attack. Both officers soon realized that, far from being on the offensive, the Left Division was about to suffer a major attack by British regulars.
From Benson Lossing, *Pictorial Field Book of the War of 1812*, New York, 1869

A View of the South Bank and Bridge of the Chippawa River, 1804
During the afternoon of 4 July 1814 Riall ordered the buildings on the south bank burned and then dropped the centre section of the bridge in the face of Scott's brigade. When he decided to attack the next day, he was forced to wait until mid-afternoon until his engineers had repaired the bridge. He then crossed the Chippawa River and assembled his army in the area of cleared fields on the south bank hidden from American view by the strip of woodland separating Chippawa from Samuel Street's farm.
Watercolour by Sempronius Stretton, 1804, courtesy National Archives of Canada, C-18826

Captain, New York State Militia, War of 1812
In contrast to the enlisted personnel, militia officers usually purchased or otherwise obtained proper uniforms. Porter's Third Brigade contained a number of New York units, as well as Pennsylvanian, Canadian, and native contingents. Although not as well trained as their regular counterparts, they performed well throughout the campaign under Porter's leadership.
Painting by H.C. McBarron, courtesy Parks Canada

CHAPTER 8

"WHY, THESE ARE REGULARS!"
Battle on the Plain - I

Winfield Scott was awake and in fine fettle when Gardner galloped up to his tent. That morning a special 4th of July dinner, "with many fine extras added" by Scott, had happily arrived by boat "to be dispatched by officers and men, who had scarcely broken fast in thirty-odd hours." But it was never Scott's way to go easy on his troops, and "to keep his men in breath" he had decided to hold "a parade for grand evolutions" that afternoon on the plain. The First Brigade was assembling for this drill when Gardner arrived.[1]

Scott had little respect for non-regular troops and was not happy when he received Brown's orders. As Colonel Charles Gardner later tactfully explained to Brown: "he had some objecting remarks – not signifying objects to obey, nor intended for your ears, but expression of his dislike to be ordered ... to support the militia when they got into difficulty." Orders being orders, though, Scott replied that "he would go out and drill his Brigade."[2]

Already assembled, the First Brigade of about thirteen-hundred strong, was soon in motion north on the river road. As the column neared the Street's Creek bridge, Brown rode up shouting: "You will have a battle!"[3] Scott retorted that he would "go out and drill, but that he did not believe he should meet three hundred of the enemy." Brown had no time to disabuse his subordinate of this notion but rode on to alert the remainder of the division. At almost the same moment, the first British artillery rounds started to land south of Street's Creek.[4]

After Pearson's regular light infantry, militia, and warriors had pursued the American force into the woods, Riall ordered the remainder of his force to march through the strip of woodland and deploy on the northern end of the plain. Lisle's dragoons led the way, followed by Lieutenant Richard Armstrong's two 24-pdr. guns and one 5.5 inch howitzer. Armstrong unlimbered on the river road about four hundred yards north of the Street's

Creek bridge. Behind the guns came the three regular infantry battalions, with the 8th Foot in the lead. The 1st and 100th Foot formed in line to the west of Armstrong's gunners with the 100th on the left near the river. On the right flank of this line, Lieutenant Edward Sheppard, RA, accompanied by Mackonochie, brought three brass 6-pdr. guns into position. As the plain was not wide enough at its northern end for Riall to deploy his three battalions abreast, he placed the 8th Foot in a separate line to the right and rear of the 1st and 100th. Finally, Lisle's squadron of light dragoons took post on the river road directly behind Armstrong's gunners. It was about 4.15 p.m.[5]

Riall had 1360 regular infantry under his command, but since he had detached the light infantry companies from three battalions, the force he marched onto the plain probably numbered about twelve hundred regulars. His troops were fairly confident, but there were some disquieting rumours floating about. In the 100th Foot, Private George Ferguson remembered it being said that the American front rank was composed of desperate men, "deserters and Europeans," who would fight to the death. Another rumour that made its way along the soldiers' informal grapevine was that, on being told that the American army outnumbered the British five to one, Riall was supposed to have replied: "O, they are a set of cowardly untrained men – scape gallows or state prison men who will not stand the bayonet."[6]

Lieutenant Colonel George Hay, commanding officer of the 100th, had only been with the Right Division for a few hours, but he was already beginning to have some doubts about its commanding general. When he was well enough to present himself to Riall, the British commander had shown him a map of the area and informed him that he intended to march straight down the river road and attack the enemy. Hay pointed out that the Americans would probably be in strength in the woods and might attack the British column on the march, but Riall paid no attention. That was exactly what had happened, although Pearson's light infantry had removed that threat. Now seated on his horse in front of his regiment, Hay could make out the line of Street's Creek, which to him appeared to be "a bank about five foot high in a straight line." He continued to worry about the woods to the west and hoped that Pearson's men would clear them of "American Kentucky riflemen."[7]

On Hay's left, beside the banks of the Niagara, Lieutenant Armstrong was estimating distances to the farm buildings directly in front of him and to the American gun positions situated beside the Street's Creek bridge. A seven-year veteran, the young officer was in command of two brass 24-pdr. guns, the most powerful field pieces in North America. Cast as experimental weapons during the reign of George II, they had been sent to Canada during the Revolutionary War and were still in service. Although their range was short, the 24-pdrs. fired an extremely heavy projectile for their size and could be expected to do deadly work against opposing infantry. Armstrong's 5.5 inch howitzer was commanded by Lieutenant Thomas Jack of the Royal Artillery Drivers who, normally in charge of the gun teams that hauled the field artillery, had this day wangled himself a combat assignment. Their weapons loaded, the two officers waited for the command to open fire.[8]

When they got it, their gunners fired the three artillery pieces which were immediately enveloped in a cloud of thick, acrid smoke as they recoiled back six to eight feet. Benjamin Ropes, whose picket, sheltering in the Ussher's house and barn, had the dubious honour to be the first British target, recalled that "the En[e]my had uncovered their Artillery" and "Comminced a full fire on our Guard."[9] Towson immediately replied with his three pieces and the battle of the plain began.[10]

As Scott's column came into view south of the Street's Creek bridge, Armstrong switched targets to bring them under fire. Happily for the First Brigade, his elevation was too high – Drummer Hanks remembered that the "balls and grape, mostly passed over our heads and fell into a bend of the river."[11] Some of the rounds landed in the camp and the surgeon of the Twenty-First Infantry was later horrified to find that one had stove in a large cask of wine stored in his tent.[12]

But Armstrong corrected his aim and the First Brigade began to take casualties. As the Twenty-Second Infantry approached the bridge, a shell burst tore off Captain Joseph Henderson's hat – an obliging soldier picked it up and returned it to him. A round shot bounced into the ranks of the Ninth Infantry and carried away part of Captain Thomas Harrison's leg, but Harrison set an example for his men who were forced to step over him. In Scott's words, he "preserved a perfect serenity under the tortures of his wound, and utterly refused any assistance till the enemy should be beaten."[13]

Marching in quick time, the brigade passed the narrow defile of the bridge and moved north on the river road directly into the fire of Armstrong's guns. Nearing the Ussher house, Scott wheeled them to the left along a farm lane that led west from the road into the plain. This lane was bordered by split rail fences, and the troops were forced to tear them down in order to enter the fields.

The infantry of the First Brigade – the combined Ninth/Twenty-Second, Eleventh, and Twenty-Fifth Infantry – were all experienced soldiers. Recruited in Massachusetts and New Hampshire, the Ninth had fought at Sackets Harbor and Crysler's Farm. They were commanded by

Major Henry Leavenworth, a thirty-one-year-old native of Delhi, New York and a peacetime lawyer who was thought to be "the ablest battalion officer in the army."[14] Attached to the Ninth was a two hundred-strong detachment of the Twenty-Second Infantry recruited from New Jersey, Delaware, and Pennsylvania, another veteran unit that had seen considerable fighting in the last two years.

Raised in Vermont and New Hampshire, the Eleventh Infantry had seen action at Crysler's Farm in 1813. Their commanding officer, Colonel Thomas B. Campbell, was a westerner who had made a reputation for himself raiding native villages on the Missineway river in 1812. He was also responsible for a destructive raid against the Long Point area of Upper Canada in April 1814.[15]

Twenty-six-year-old Major Thomas Sydney Jesup from Kentucky commanded the Twenty-Fifth Infantry, recruited in Connecticut, Rhode Island, and Vermont and which had fought at Fort George, Sackets Harbor, and Crysler's Farm.[16]

Leavenworth's Ninth and Twenty-Second Infantry formed in line immediately to the west of the barn, while Campbell's Eleventh deployed in a similar formation some distance to their left. Jesup was preparing to place his Twenty-Fifth on Campbell's left when he received orders from Scott "to go to the extreme left and be governed by circumstances," as the brigade commander could see that Pearson's light infantry had reached the area of the fence that bordered the western extremity of the plain.[17]

To continue covering the same extent of frontage, Scott then ordered Campbell to extend the interval between his regiment and Leavenworth's to a fourfold distance. Rather than face to the left and move by ranks, Campbell probably opted to move obliquely forward and away from Leavenworth, leaving his regiment some distance closer to the British line. Wanting to get into the action, Ropes hauled his picket out of their shelter and formed on the left of the Ninth/Twenty-Second in the interval vacated by Campbell.[18]

Although under constant artillery fire, the brigade's deployment was carried out quickly and without confusion. Towson returned the British fire. The thirty-year-old Maryland native had waited until the First Brigade cleared the bridge, then limbering up his two 6-pdr. guns and 5.5 howitzer, moved north to come into action on the river road to the right of Leavenworth.[19]

The battle now became a gunners' duel. But, while Armstrong and Jack targeted Towson, Sheppard, positioned on the right flank of the 1st Foot, concentrated his three guns on the Twenty-Fifth Infantry. He could clearly see that the American regiment, which was in column formation, presented an attractive target. Sheppard's gun detachments fired with murderous efficiency, shooting the standard round a minute for light pieces and probably, given that the range was over five hundred yards, using round shot in preference to canister. The British artillery commander, Mackonochie, who was on the field but left his subordinates to carry out their duties, later reported that: "I cannot conceive it possible for Officers and Men to behave better; no hurry or confusion was observable."[20]

Armstrong and Jack's gunners, meanwhile, duelled with their American opposite numbers in Towson's company. For artillery, the two sides were firing at extremely close range, and Mackonochie could only attribute the small number of casualties suffered by his gunners to "the very indifferent fire of the Enemy's artillery, their elevation being in general too high."[21] Even so, a shell from Towson's howitzer exploded a British ammunition limber, killing two team horses and disabling one of the 24-pdr. guns. A few minutes later, the American howitzer was put out of action.[22]

Riall and his staff had watched as Scott's brigade crossed the bridge over Street's Creek. Noting the grey uniforms, they at first decided that the Americans were militia wearing the grey homespun wool common to farmers throughout North America. Then, as the American deployed without faltering under heavy fire, they changed their minds – "Why, these are regulars!" Riall is said to have exclaimed.[23] Private Ferguson and his comrades in the 100th came to the same conclusion, deciding that the Americans facing them were "unquestionably well disciplined troops."[24]

Well trained or not, the only opponents Riall could see in front of him was Scott's thirteen-hundred and Towson's three artillery pieces. These numbers accorded with his own intelligence that a major part of Brown's army was still occupied besieging Fort Erie. Having watched American militia run away from British regulars the previous December, Riall had little respect for the military abilities of "Cousin Jonathan," and the numbers being about equal, he was confident that the superior discipline of his regulars would prevail, as it had in the past. He decided to attack.

Ordering the 1st and 100th "to charge the enemy in front," Riall directed the 8th Foot to advance "to the right" to counter Jesup's Twenty-Fifth Infantry, which he could see in column to the west of Scott's line.[25] These orders received, the battalion commanders repeated them to their units and the British line moved forward. It was about 4:30 p.m.

Being the main defensive and offensive formation of the British army in 1814, the line was the subject of much attention in its manual. This manual stipulated that a distance of one pace (two and a half feet) was to be maintained between the two ranks of the line as the "constant and habitual order at which troops are at all times formed and moved." The men in

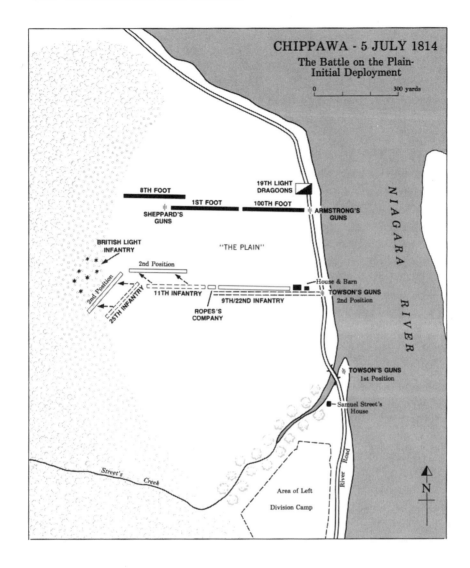

CHIPPAWA - 5 JULY 1814

The Battle on the Plain-
Initial Deployment

0   300 yards

19TH LIGHT
DRAGOONS

8TH FOOT

1ST FOOT   100TH FOOT

SHEPPARD'S   ARMSTRONG'S
GUNS   GUNS

BRITISH LIGHT
INFANTRY   "THE PLAIN"

2nd Position

2nd Position   House & Barn

2nd Position

11TH INFANTRY   TOWSON'S GUNS
25TH INFANTRY   2nd Position

9TH/22ND INFANTRY

ROPES'S
COMPANY

TOWSON'S GUNS
1st Position

Samuel Street's
House

Street's   Creek

Area of Left
Division Camp

N I A G A R A   R I V E R

River Road

N

Map 3
Chippawa – 5 July 1814: The Battle on the Plain – Initial Deployment

1. British Major General Phineas Riall deploys on the northern end of the plain with Lieutenant Colonel George Hay's 100th Regiment of Foot on his left, or east flank, near the Niagara River, Lieutenant Colonel John Gordon's 1st Foot in line to their right, and the 8th Foot under Major Thomas Evans in a separate line to their right rear. Lieutenant Armstrong, RA, positions his three pieces of artillery on the river road in line with the 100th and 1st Foot. Lieutenant Sheppard, RA, also positions his three guns in line with these two units to the immediate right, or west, of the 1st Foot. The 19th Light Dragoons take position to the immediate rear of Armstrong's artillery.

2. Under fire from the British artillery, American Brigadier General Winfield Scott's First Brigade moves from the American camp across the bridge over Street's Creek. American artillery Captain Nathan Towson, positioned between the bridge and the river, on the south bank of the creek, returns this fire with his three field pieces.

3. Still under artillery fire, Scott marches his brigade north on the river road to the farm lane near the Ussher's house and barn. He then wheels into the lane and moves west along it to reach a point where his brigade can deploy into line to face the British line.

4. Scott deploys his troops. Major Henry Leavenworth forms his combined Ninth/Twenty-Second Infantry in line north of the lane and to the immediate left of the Ussher's barn. Captain Benjamin Ropes takes his company of the Twenty-First Infantry, which has been on picket in the area of the Ussher's farm throughout the day, and forms on the right of Leavenworth. Colonel Thomas B. Campbell forms his Eleventh Infantry to the left of Ropes's company. After the infantry have turned off the river road, Towson moves his three artillery pieces forward to take a position on the road beside the Ussher house and fires at Armstrong's British guns.

5. Just as Major Thomas S. Jesup is about to form his Twenty-Fifth Infantry in line to the left or west of the Eleventh, Scott orders him to take up a position on the far left. Seeing the three companies of British regular light infantry in the tree line of the woods bordering the plain, Jesup forms his regiment facing them. He has exposed his right flank to the fire of Sheppard's three British artillery pieces and suffers heavy casualties.

6. To increase the breadth of his line, Scott orders Campbell's Eleventh Infantry to increase the interval between it and Leavenworth's regiment. Campbell moves forward obliquely to the northwest and his final position is slightly advanced from the line formed by Leavenworth's Ninth/Twenty-Second and Ropes's company.

these ranks were packed close together, each soldier occupying a space, by regulation, twenty-two inches wide – so that a man "could feel with his elbow the touch of his neighbour."[26]

In the centre of each battalion marched the colour party, consisting of two ensigns, the most junior rank of infantry officer, each carrying a "colour" or flag. There were two of these devices: the King's Colour, basically the Union Standard embellished with the regimental number, and the Regimental Colour, whose field matched the facings of the regiments – blue for the 1st and deep yellow for the 100th. Marching forward at the regulation measure of seventy-five paces to the minute, halting at frequent intervals to maintain their dressing, using the position of the colours as a guide, the red-coated regulars trampled down Samuel Street's crops as they moved toward the waiting Americans.

Having told his battalion commanders what to do, Riall wisely did not tell them how to do it, but positioned himself and his aides some distance behind the advancing infantry to keep an eye on all aspects of the battle.

Lieutenant Colonel John Gordon of the 1st Foot and Hay of the 100th, both mounted, rode in front of their units. Their orders were "to charge the enemy in front," and to accomplish this they would utilize a combination of fire and shock. They would close Scott's brigade without firing, saving that crucial, properly-loaded first round, until within good musketry range. The two battalions would then fire two or three disciplined volleys and follow them up with a quick advance with the bayonet. This simple but effective tactic had worked well in Europe and had been used with positive results against American regulars the previous autumn at Crysler's Farm.

To the right and rear of the 1st and 100th, the 8th Foot also moved forward. As the battalions moved, they blocked Sheppard's line of vision so that he was forced to cease firing, and British artillery support was reduced to Armstrong's remaining 24-pdr. gun and Jack's howitzer. Both pieces continued to fire at Towson's guns, some four hundred yards straight down the river road.

The three British battalions were solid, veteran units. In existence since 1633, the 1st (or the Royal Scots) Regiment of Foot was the senior line infantry unit of the army and revelled in its nickname "Pontius Pilate's Bodyguard." It had been sent to Canada in late 1812, following service in the West Indies, and had seen action as marines on Lake Ontario and at the storming of Fort Niagara in December 1813.[27]

The 8th (or King's) Regiment of Foot were old Canadian hands who had seen considerable service during the war, fighting at Ogdensburg, York, Sackets Harbor, Fort George, Stoney Creek, and on the Niagara the previous December. Commanded by thirty-seven-year-old Major Thomas Evans, a veteran of the West Indies and Egypt who had been in North America since 1805. The 8th Foot had a good record.[28]

The 100th (or His Royal Highness the Prince Regent's County of Dublin) Regiment, having been in existence only since 1805, was not so nearly as august as the 1st and 8th Foot. An Irish unit, it had acquired a good fighting reputation based on sheer Emerald Isle *élan*. The 100th had fought at Sackets Harbor and had particularly distinguished itself during a raid on Black Rock, NY, and at the storming of Fort Niagara in 1813.[29]

In the red-coated ranks moving forward that summer afternoon were soldiers like Sergeant James Commins of the 8th Foot, a veteran of every major action that regiment had fought during the war and a man who despised his enemy. But Commins had heard some of the rumours about superior American strength and thought that Riall was engaging on "disadvantageous terms."[30] In Captain John Smyth's No. 6 Company of the 1st Foot, Sergeant Hay Fenton, a nineteen-year veteran, probably ignored these rumours, if he heard them. Most likely, from his position in the rank of file closers marching behind the two fighting ranks, he was keeping an eye on the greener members of his company, such as twenty-six-year-old Private Abram Fearon from Christchurch in Middlesex, who had just completed his first year of service. In the ranks of the 100th Foot was Ferguson, that God-fearing man but improbable soldier. He later confessed that he only fired in anger once during the war and was certain that he didn't hit anyone. Still, although he had permission to be away from his regiment, Ferguson was with them that sweltering July day.[31]

Not all the British and Canadians were eager to get into combat. Lieutenant Michael O'Flanagan of the 8th Foot lagged behind as his unit advanced and then laid on the ground before disappearing. Captain William Brereton, commanding No. 3 Company of the 1st Foot also fell behind and his company went into action led by its senior subaltern. Ferguson remembered seeing "some professed Loyalists and brave soldiers hiding themselves behind logs, or the bank or running into the woods."[32]

But these were exceptions and the greater number of men in the ranks moved forward to do their duty. They marched in silence as standing orders in the Right Division forbade talking or shouting in action lest it "reduce us to the level of our opponents."[33] They were sweating in their thick, wool coatees and most were thirsty, as it was the warmest part of a hot July day. But there was no hesitation as they neared the grey-uniformed enemy they could see to their front.

Watching that silent, imperturbable line of infantry coming closer, Scott made ready. As the British advanced, he spotted something – what had appeared to have been a continuous line of enemy infantry across the north end of the plain now separated into two distinct elements. The 1st and 100th were coming directly toward him but the 8th was in a separate line some distance behind them. If the two elements of the British line continued to move apart, the frontage occupied by Scott's line, deployed on the wider southern end of the plain and broadened still further by the increased interval between the Ninth and Eleventh Regiments, would exceed that of the oncoming 1st and 100th. Scott would thus outflank on the west the two British units, a distinct tactical advantage. Seeing an opportunity, Scott rode to Campbell's Eleventh Infantry on his left.

He arrived to find it under command of Major John McNeil, as Campbell had been wounded by artillery fire and had been forced to leave the field. Scott wasted no time in ordering McNeil to throw forward his left so as to take the flank of the oncoming British line under fire. McNeil, a thirty-year-old native of New Hampshire, immediately obeyed these orders.[34]

Riding back along the front of his brigade, the tall Virginian took the opportunity to boost his men's spirits, and remembering the 4th of July dinner they had just consumed, shouted at them "to make a new anniversary!"[35]

Scott's next stop was Towson's gunners engaged in their private war with their British counterparts. Towson was suffering from an eye infection, and in the smoke and confusion of his duel with the British artillery, had not realized that the British infantry were moving forward. Scott ordered the gunner to change targets and then rode back to his infantry.[36]

Just before the British came within musket range, he made an additional effort to buck up his men by calling out: "The enemy say that Americans are good at long shot; but cannot stand the cold iron. I call upon you instantly to give the lie to the slander!"[37]

A few seconds later, when the British had advanced to about one hundred and fifty to two hundred feet from the American line, Scott gave the order to fire.[38]

Scott Directs His Artillery to Change Targets, 5 July 1814
As the British infantry neared his brigade, Scott rode to Captain Nathan
Towson's gunners on his right flank and requested Towson to switch targets
from the enemy artillery to the enemy infantry. Although the uniforms in this
nineteenth-century print are inaccurate, the clouds of powder smoke that
obscure the gun position give an indication of the poor visibility on a
Napoleonic-period battlefield.
From David Strother, *An Illustrated Life of General Winfield Scott*, New York, 1847

British Infantryman, 1814

In the late afternoon of 5 July 1814, three British regiments advanced in line against Winfield Scott's First Brigade. Seasoned veterans who had beaten American regulars in a dozen actions, they were confident that they would be successful. When they came within musket range, it was the intention of their regimental commanders to halt, dress their lines, fire several rapid and concentrated volleys of musketry and then advance quickly with the bayonet.

Painting by G.A. Embleton, courtesy Parks Canada

Major John McNeil, Eleventh Infantry, U.S. Army (1784-1859)

John McNeil entered the American army as a captain in 1812 and, on the afternoon of 5 July 1814, assumed command of the Eleventh Infantry when its colonel was wounded in the opening moments of the battle on the plain. His biggest problem was not the British but his new horse, which having never experienced gunfire was nearly uncontrollable with fear. For his actions during the battle, McNeil would earn brevet promotion to lieutenant colonel.

From Benson Lossing, *Pictorial Field Book of the War of 1812*, New York, 1869

National Colour, Eleventh Infantry, U.S. Army
This colour was carried by the regiment at the battle of Chippawa, 5 July 1814.
It has a dark blue field, light blue scroll, and gold edging and lettering. As regimental colours were often visible above the smoke of battle, they made useful aiming points for enemy fire and the task of carrying them was a hazardous one usually accorded to very junior officers.
Courtesy West Point Museum, U.S. Military Academy

The "Plain," 1993

Drummer boy Jarvis Hanks of the Eleventh Infantry recalled the open field or plain north of Street's Creek as being covered on the day of battle by "grass about three feet high and very thrifty." This photograph, which looks east to the Niagara River, shows the area where the British 1st and 100th Foot made contact with Winfield Scott's First Brigade on 5 July 1814. It has changed little in the intervening 179 years.

Photograph by Robert Foley, 5 July 1993

View from Street's (Ussher's) Creek Looking North, 1993

On the right is the river road that follows the bank of the Niagara River. To the left in the middle distance can be seen the "Plain" where the heaviest fighting of the battle took place.

Photograph by Robert Foley, 5 July 1993

View of the Bridge over Street's (Ussher's) Creek, 1993
This photograph looking south shows the modern bridge over the creek and
the thick bushes that demarcate the line of the stream coming in from the west.
Street's Creek provided both cover for British snipers during the morning of
5 July 1814 and an obstacle to American manoeuvre during the afternoon.
Photograph by Robert Foley, 5 July 1993

Mouth of Street's (Ussher's) Creek, 1993
The photograph, looking north, shows the mouth of the creek as it empties into
the Niagara. In 1814, the creek was wider and deeper. On the left is the river
road that parallels the Niagara River. On the afternoon of 5 July 1814, Towson's
gunners duelled with their British counterparts by firing straight up and down
this road.
Photograph by Robert Foley, 5 July 1993

Drummer, British Infantry Regiment 1814
As the 1st and 100th Foot neared the American line during the afternoon of 5 July 1814, they were accompanied by their drummers. In the British army in 1814, drummers not only acted as signallers in camp and in the field but also had the unpleasant task of inflicting corporal punishment. For this reason, they were often grown men.
Watercolour by Barry Rich, courtesy Parks Canada

CHAPTER 9

"THE SLAUGHTER WAS GREAT"
Battle on the Plain - II

The ranks of the First Brigade were shrouded in a thick cloud of dirty smoke as they opened a concentrated volley of musketry at the British line. From his position on the river road, Towson joined in the fray by firing canister obliquely through the red-coated formation from his two remaining pieces. Hit by the force of that fire, the 1st and 100th Foot came to a standstill. Their ranks, momentarily disarranged by the dead and wounded, appeared to waver, but discipline and training asserted themselves and both battalions were steadied as the casualties were hauled clear of the line, and officers and sergeants moved the survivors into the centre.

Seeing that the Americans intended to make a fight of it, Hay and Gordon ordered their men to return fire. Apparently this was done by both ranks of both units – Ferguson of the 100th remembered that the "whole line received the order to fire a volley."[1] Now the British were blinded by powder smoke and deafened by the noise of their own discharges as, in Ropes's words, "the action became general." The time was about 4:45 p.m.[2]

Once started, the opposing lines continued to exchange volleys at close range. The companies on the left or westernmost flank of the Eleventh Infantry, which had been thrown forward on Scott's orders, inflicted heavy casualties on the British right flank. Scott later reported that the fire of McNeil's regiment "was most effective from the oblique position which his corps judiciously occupied."[3]

But McNeil was having his problems. The noise and smoke were too much for his horse, a new acquisition and unused to battle. Having trouble controlling the prancing, terrified animal, which threatened to remove both itself and its rider from the action, McNeil dismounted and gave the unruly beast a good swat on its rump, sending it racing to safety in the rear. Now a true infantryman, he resumed command of his regiment as volley followed volley.[4]

Towson's fire was very effective. Each canister round from his two 6-pdr. guns, containing thirty to forty lead bullets, tore into the ranks of the 100th Foot, the closest British unit. Second Lieutenant Edward Randolph of Brown's staff, who had volunteered to assist Towson during the action, watched as "breaches" or gaps were blown through the opposing line, but he noted that these breaches "were soon filled up" as the Irish regiment closed its ranks.[5] However, the effect of the American artillery fire was disastrous for Lieutenant George Lyon's grenadier company, stationed on the 100th's left flank almost opposite Towson's guns. It was a "scene of carnage" remembered Lieutenant John Stevenson as men fell beside him "like hail."[6]

Despite their casualties, the British battalions held their ground and stubbornly returned the heavy American fire. On both sides long hours of drill paid dividends as men fired on command and automatically reloaded. To save time, most disdained priming their pieces and simply rammed the charge, wad, and ball hard down the bores of their muskets, and then banged the butts hard on the ground to shake powder out of the vent into the pan. Known as "loading with running ball," this procedure allowed them to fire faster. Sergeant Eliah T. Bond of the Eleventh Infantry came up with a more novel means of increasing his rate of fire – Drummer Jarvis Hanks, his drum slung over his shoulder, held Bond's ramrod between shots. "By this method," the teenager proudly remembered, "considerable time was saved."[7]

Both sides suffered heavily, but given the added effect of Towson's artillery and McNeil's flanking position, the British took more casualties. "The slaughter was great," remembered Ferguson of the 100th Foot, "They fell on my right and left."[8] Lieutenant George Williams's premonition came partly true; he was wounded, but not fatally. In both lines, the dead and wounded were dragged to the rear, and the remaining soldiers closed ranks. Blinded and choked by smoke, crazed with thirst and fear, seeing comrades falling around them and hearing the screams of the wounded, the red-coated British and grey-jacketed American infantry fired and loaded, fired and loaded.

From their gun positions, the British artillery officers, Lieutenants Edward Sheppard, Thomas Jack, and Richard Armstrong, watched helplessly as their infantry brethren slugged it out with the Americans. They were not able to render as much support as they would have liked, because the infantry's advance had blocked their line of fire. Armstrong and Jack, therefore, concentrated on Towson's artillery. But the American guns, presenting a frontage of approximately forty square feet each and obscured by smoke, were difficult targets to hit. Towson took casualties though – nearly a fifth of his company was killed or wounded. In desperation Armstrong and Jack advanced their pieces until they were two hundred yards away from their target. At such close range, they came under fire from Scott's infantry. Luckily for the gunners, the American fire was inaccurate. Mackonochie later reported that the gunners' "escape from the effects of Musquetry I look upon as the fortune of War."[9]

While Scott was engaged on the plain, the remainder of the Left Division prepared to support him. By the time Brown rode into camp, Ripley had assembled his Second Brigade, and they were formed up "resting on their arms." Brown ordered Gardner to guide Ripley and his best unit, the Twenty-First Infantry, across the upper reaches of Street's Creek "and through the edge of the thin wood bordering the plain" in order "to take the enemy in the flank and assist in the battle."[10] Ripley moved out, but had great difficulty getting his men across the creek, which was chest deep. He was then further delayed by the dense undergrowth north of the stream. Marching in the ranks of the Twenty-First was Joseph Treat – a captain that morning, he was now a volunteer private.[11]

Mounted on a "gaily caparisoned" horse that he had found running riderless through the camp, Porter rallied the survivors of his Third Brigade. He augmented them with the two hundred Pennsylvanians who had remained behind and reorganized ready for action. Meanwhile, many of his warriors, taking fresh heart, went back into the woods to skirmish with the enemy.[12]

Major Jacob Hindman, the divisional artillery commander, requested Brown's permission to bring up the rest of his artillery, but was told that it "would be required for a different scene."[13] After the gunner pressed him, Brown relented, and soon Captain John Ritchie's company, with two 6-pdr. guns and a 5.5 inch howitzer, and a 12-pdr. gun from Captain Thomas Biddle's company under Lieutenant James Hall, were ordered across the creek to support the First Brigade.[14]

Satisfied with these arrangements, Brown returned with his staff to the plain. Riding to the western flank of Scott's line, the American commander hoped to assist Jesup and the Twenty-Fifth Infantry, who appeared to be having troubles.[15]

By the time he got there, Jesup, an independent and self-reliant officer, had solved his own problems. After being detached to the left, Jesup had advanced along the farm lane and halted about 150 yards from the rail fence that bordered the western edge of the plain. Behind this fence were the three regular British light infantry companies that had worked their way down from the Chippawa. They opened a brisk fire on the Twenty-Fifth, and Jesup, redeploying his regiment from column to line, faced the fence and returned fire. He was then hit on his right flank by Sheppard's three 6-pdrs. and lost fifty men in the space of ten minutes.[16]

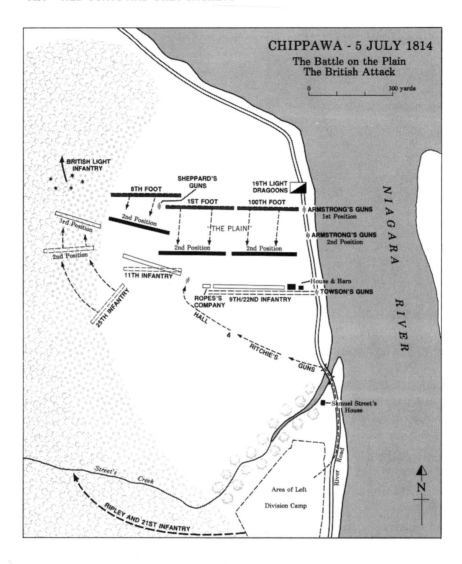

Map 4
Chippawa – 5 July 1814: The Battle on the Plain – The British Attack

1. On Riall's order, Hay and Gordon move their regiments forward in line to engage the American First Brigade deployed on the southern part of the plain. In their rear, Evans moves the 8th Foot forward. As the British infantry advance, they obstruct their gunners' lines of fire. So that he can render effective support, Armstrong moves his three field pieces south on the river road.

2. As the 1st and 100th Foot approach, Scott orders Campbell to throw forward the Eleventh Infantry's left flank to catch the oncoming British line in enfilade. When the two oncoming British units come within effective musket range, Scott orders Campbell, Leavenworth, and Towson to open fire. They do so, the 1st and 100th Foot come to a halt and return the fire.

3. Jesup, meanwhile, attacks the British light infantry in the skirt of the wood with his Twenty-Fifth Infantry. They fall back and Jesup pursues them north, moving in the semi-cleared area at the edge of the plain. As he advances, he catches the 8th Foot in the flank and forces Evans to gradually withdraw. The 8th Foot is thus unable to support the main British attack.

4. While the musketry duel continues on the plain, Major General Jacob Brown orders Brigadier General Eleazar Ripley to take his best unit, the Twenty-First Infantry, in an outflanking movement through the woods to catch the British line in the flank. Ripley moves out but his progress is delayed by the depth of Street's Creek and the underbrush. At the same time, with Brown's permission, Major Jacob Hindman, the American artillery commander, orders Captain Ritchie and Lieutenant Hall to move their artillery pieces forward from the camp to support Scott. Hall and Ritchie take position in the interval between Ropes's company of the Twenty-First and Campbell's Eleventh Infantry.

5. After a short but vicious and bloody musketry duel, Riall orders Hay and Gordon to retreat. In good order, the 1st and 100th Foot move north up the plain, and although harassed by American cavalry, the entire British force withdraws safely to the north bank of the Chippawa River.

"Finding the showers of shot and shell so destructive as the Enemy so completely covered as to render my fire almost useless," Jesup ordered his men to shoulder arms and advance on the light infantry.[17] As Captain George Howard later wrote, the Twenty-Fifth came "within grinning distance," then Jesup gave the commands: "halt: ready: fire three rounds and charge!"[18] Before the smoke had cleared, the Americans moved forward to see the light infantry fall back into the woods.

Jesup now reformed in the skirt of the woods on the far side of the fence and followed the enemy north. In his words: "The Enemy retreated on our approach through the wood and we pursued him so rapidly that we gained the flank of a strong detachment posted in a field on our right."[19] This was Major Thomas Evans's 8th Foot that had been ordered by Riall to advance in line against the Twenty-Fifth. Detaching Captain Daniel Ketchum's company to keep the light infantry occupied, Jesup changed front and fired into Evans's flank.

The experienced Evans withdrew the 8th north on the plain to a new position but Jesup, advancing under cover of the fence, again fired on the flank of the British unit. Evans was forced to pull back again, but at that moment Ketchum asked Jesup for help, as Riall's light infantry had rallied and counter-attacked with superior numbers. Changing front again, Jesup advanced to support his captain whereupon the light infantry "fled on our approach, which terminated the action on the left."[20] This private war, however, prevented the 8th Foot from supporting the other two British battalions in their attack on Scott's line.

Meanwhile, the two opposing lines continued to exchange musketry fire. For the First Brigade, the long weeks of hard work at Flint Hill began to pay off as they loaded and fired without cease. Leavenworth and McNeil steadied their units as casualties were taken – a participant later recalled that the latter "formed his regiment under the fire of the enemy, with the accuracy of a parade, and ... every word of command he gave could be distinctly heard far beyond his own line."[21] In the ranks of the Twenty-Second Infantry, Henderson had his third close call when a large soldier in front of him was killed by a shell fragment and fell over backward, knocking Henderson to the ground.[22]

Despite the smoke and the inherent inaccuracy of their weapons, many of Scott's infantry were using aimed fire and their targets were the British officers they could see along the British line. In the 100th Foot, Lieutenant John Stevenson knew "not except under the mercy and Kindness of Almighty God how I escaped" although he "was slightly wounded in the fingers of his left hand by a musket shot." His fellow officers did not enjoy the same fortune – writing after the battle, Stevenson compiled a grim list:

Captain Thomas Sherrard "received three balls in him"; Captain William Sleigh was "dangerously wounded in the groin"; Lieutenant John Valentine "in both legs"; Lieutenant Francis Fortune "in the shoulder and leg," and Ensign John Clark "in the foot."[23] Of the seventeen officers who marched onto the plain with the 100th Foot, only four were still on their feet towards the close of the action. Things were only marginally better in the 1st Foot, which had ten officers killed and wounded.[24]

True to their personal code, however, the officers continued to provide examples of behaviour to their men. When a company commander was hit, his most senior subordinate replaced him and if that man went down, the next senior until, finally, a sergeant would step forward. It is not known whether Sergeant Hay Fenton of the 1st Foot ever assumed command of his company; in any case, Fenton no longer had to concern himself with the steadiness of Private Abram Fearon – both men were dead.[25]

The American line remained firm and Hay and Gordon knew they had to close with the enemy. But despite all their exhortations, their men were unwilling to move forward. Here and there, a company commander was able to get his men to advance, and to some American participants it appeared that the British were "preparing to charge."[26] But the weight of the American fire was too much, and these companies fell back. A highly visible target, Gordon took a musket ball in the mouth, and unable to give orders, had to be escorted off the field. Despite all my efforts, Hay later wrote, "I could not get them to advance."[27]

In desperation, he rode to his elite company, Lyon's grenadiers, on the left near the Niagara, to get them to lead a charge. Before Lyon could comply with this order, he was knocked to the ground by a canister bullet that "went through his right thigh a few inches above the knee."[28] Hay then turned to the next senior officer, Lieutenant Patrick Gibbons, but Gibbons and Ensign John Rea, the third officer of the company, were both killed before his eyes. Hay's turn was not long in coming – a musket ball severed the Achilles' tendon of his good leg and he had to be led away on his horse.[29]

Unwilling to advance, unwilling to retreat, the red-coated infantry continued to fire, and to take casualties. Private Ferguson was hit in the arm, "but knew nothing of it until my piece fell out of my hand, and I saw the blood running down in a stream." Faint with pain, he fell out of the ranks and made his way back up the plain. Although he was moving away from danger, Ferguson disliked being apart from his comrades as "it seemed more dangerous leaving the field than even in it."[30]

Coming to the wagons that had been brought forward to carry away the wounded, an officer, seeing Ferguson's wound, bound it up with the private's own handkerchief. Suffering "much, from want of water, the day being exceedingly hot," Ferguson asked his Samaritan for water, but only received an offer of rum. Although he was a devout teetotaller, these were exceptional circumstances, and Ferguson drank to find "a partial relief – the only time I ever experienced any benefit from spiritous liquors."[31]

As Ritchie's and Hall's artillery pieces crossed the bridge, Brown directed them to the space between McNeil's Eleventh and Leavenworth's Ninth/Twenty-Second Regiments. Moving along the farm lane, they unlimbered and went into action, joining Towson in firing canister into the British ranks. Watching the effect, Scott concluded that it "was not in human nature that a conflict like this should last many seconds."[32]

And it didn't. First, the flanks of the British line began to edge back and then the centre began to waver – seeing it was no use, Riall ordered a withdrawal. He had not interfered with his subordinates' conduct of the battle, but had ridden with his staff within musket range of the Americans. His aide, Captain Samuel Holland, was wounded, and Riall himself had a bullet through his coat. The vicious firefight between the two opposing lines had lasted approximately twenty to twenty-five minutes.[33]

Maintaining their formation, the 1st and 100th Foot slowly retraced their steps to the north end of the plain. When they were out of musket range, the two battalions formed in column of march and moved north on the river road through the strip of woodland, their withdrawal was covered by the 8th Foot and Lisle's dragoons. Some of the troopers harnessed their horses to Armstrong's disabled 24-pdr. gun and got it safely away.[34]

Seeing an opportunity to create some havoc, Captain Samuel Harris brought his light dragoons onto the plain, but they were careful not to come within close range of the British rearguard. Unmolested, the Right Division crossed the bridge over the Chippawa and when the last files had reached the north bank, the engineers again dropped the centre section in the river. "John Bull," recorded one American, was now "safe from Brother Jonathan."[35]

So quickly was the withdrawal carried out that some of the native parties in the woods were nearly caught on the wrong side of the Chippawa. Captain Samuel White, the Pennsylvanian who had earlier been taken prisoner by British warriors during the fighting in the woods, had some harrowing moments during the closing moments of the battle. His captors were trotting him through pine woods when "an Indian in the rear suddenly whooped loudly, raised his rifle, and shot Col. Bull [an American prisoner] through the body" and then "sunk his tomahawk in his head, scalped him, and left his body where he fell."

Not wanting to suffer the same fate, White allowed himself to be "hurried forward, exerting all my nerve, fearing that if I failed or fell, the tomahawk, the sound of which still ran in my ears, would soon give me my quietus." He was exhausted by the time his party came in sight of the bridge over the Chippawa "just as the last of the [British] rear guard had got on it," and the American artillery started firing at the north bank. A round shot "fell within a yard of me as I pressed forward, making the clay fall all over us, and then bounded into the creek." White got across just before the bridge "was cut down."[36]

John Norton and his detachment of warriors were deep in the woods when they heard the "bugle sound a retreat." They had spent a frustrating time trying to get through the dense woods and the American warriors to attack the American camp from the west. Withdrawing as swiftly as possible, they arrived at the bridge only to find it "demolished, excepting a Log or two which yet remained." Norton called for a canoe to take his men over, but when this was not forthcoming, he was able to get them across on "the Logs remaining at the Bridge."[37]

As the smoke from the last vollies on the plain cleared, Winfield Scott watched the British pull back. He ordered an immediate advance, and the First Brigade, preceded by Harris's dragoons and followed by the artillery, moved forward over a battlefield "strewed with the Red Coated Gentry."[38] Traversing the strip of woodland and approaching the south bank of the Chippawa, they came under furious fire from British batteries on the north bank.

Scott ordered his men to lie down in their ranks with their heads toward the enemy and waited for the rest of the division. Porter, arriving a few minutes later, took up a similar recumbent position on Scott's left. Many of his militia now experienced their first artillery fire, which one thought "a new but not a very pleasant sight."[39] Recognizing Porter's fine horse, McNeil asked for, and got, his mount back.[40]

Brown then arrived with Ripley's brigade and the remainder of Hindman's artillery. The American commander had watched the climax of the battle of the plain and had been hoping that Ripley would come up in time to finish off the British. But it was not until after the British retreat that he saw Gardner emerge from the woods. He rode "in great eagerness" toward him and Gardner remembered later that Brown was in "exhilaration at the state of the battle" and urged him "to hasten Ripley's Brigade by every means in my power." In reply, Gardner pointed to the woods from which the leading elements of the Twenty-First Infantry were emerging, but "it was too late, as the brigade of Genl. Scott had broken the enemy's line, and finally put him to rout."[41]

By the time Brown got up to the Chippawa River, Scott's and Porter's men had been under artillery fire for nearly thirty minutes. He decided to bring up all his "ordnance and force the place by a direct attack" and dispatched Major Eleazar Wood and his other aide, Captain Loring Austin, to reconnoitre the British position. It took time for them to report back, and Brown, induced by their report "and the lateness of the hour," decided "to retire to camp." It was about 6:30 p.m. and the battle was over.[42]

"These are Regulars!": Winfield Scott's First Brigade, 5 July 1814
Wearing grey jackets instead of the more common blue uniforms, Scott's
brigade advances under British artillery fire on the afternoon of 5 July 1814.
Note the visibility of the regimental colours; units aligned themselves on their
colours while manoeuvring, and commanding officers stationed themselves near
the colours so that messengers could easily find them in battle.
Painting by H.C. McBarron, courtesy U.S. Army Center of Military History

View of the "Plain" Looking West, 1993
Scott's First Brigade formed in line with their right flank stationed approximately
where the photographer was standing. To the west can be seen the tree line of
the woods where Porter's brigade fought the British light infantry, native warriors, and Canadian militia. The ground has changed remarkably little in the
intervening years. Beneath this field lie the remains of nearly two hundred American, British, and Canadian soldiers, as well as native warriors from both sides.
Photograph by Robert Foley, 5 July 1993.

View of the "Plain" Looking Northwest, 1993
This view shows the area over which Riall's infantry advanced to close with
Scott's line. The woods on the left of the picture join with a "strip of woodland"
that is still in existence, 179 years after the battle. The battlefield of Chippawa
is possibly the most pristine musket-period battle site in eastern North America.
Photograph by Robert Foley, 5 July 1993

The High Point of the Battle on the "Plain"
An imaginative nineteenth-century woodcut shows Scott's brigade charging and breaking the British line. Such an event never occurred; the British line, unable to advance in the face of heavy and accurate American musketry, recoiled and withdrew slowly in good order.
From David Strother, *An Illustrated Life of General Scott*, New York, 1847

Brigadier General Eleazar W. Ripley, U.S. Army (1782-1839)
Commanding the Second Brigade, Ripley was ordered by Brown to ford Street's Creek and to attack the British flank. His movement was delayed because the stream had become almost impassible on account of past heavy rainfall, and his brigade did not enter the battle until Scott's brigade had decisively rebuffed the British attack.
Courtesy Hood Museum of Art, Dartmouth College, N.H.

Plan of an American Iron 12-pdr. Field Gun and Carriage
Towards the end of the action on the plain, Hindman brought a gun of this cali-
bre into action on the plain where it decimated the British ranks with canister.
The artillery of both sides was well served during the battle and inflicted heavy
casualties on their opponents.
From Louis de Tousard, *American Artillerist's Companion*, Philadelphia, 1812

**Major Henry Leavenworth, Ninth
Infantry, U.S. Army (1783-1834)**
Leavenworth's combined
Ninth/Twenty-Second Infantry
opposed the 100th Foot during the
battle and inflicted heavy casualties
on the British unit with accurate
musketry. Leavenworth gained
brevet promotion to lieutenant
colonel for his actions at Chippawa.
This is a postwar portrait.
Courtesy Frontier Army Museum, Fort
Leavenworth, Kansas

Major Thomas S. Jesup, Twenty-Fifth Infantry, U.S. Army (1788-1860)
Jesup commanded the Twenty-Fifth Infantry during the battle, and while the remainder of the First Brigade repulsed the main British attack, he fought a nearly independent action against the British light infantry and the 8th Foot. Promoted for his services at Chippawa, Jesup was wounded four times at the battle of Lundy's Lane, three weeks later, but would serve in the American army until 1860, reaching the rank of general.
Used with the permission of the Washington National Cathedral

Regimental Colour of the Twenty-Fifth Infantry, 1855
Carried at Chippawa and Lundy's Lane, its battle-scarred condition and broken staff attest to the ferocity of the fighting at both actions. This flag was yellow or buff in colour with a blue scroll and gold embellishment.
From Benson Lossing, *Pictorial Field Book of the War of 1812*, New York, 1869

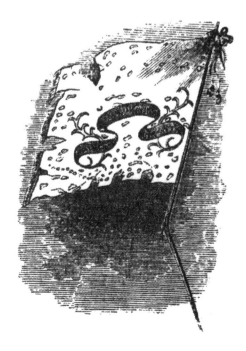

CHAPTER 10

"IT WAS PAINFUL TO WITNESS THE DISTRESS AND AGONY"
The Aftermath

From the time that Porter's men first entered the woods to "scour" them of the British to the disappearance of the last American soldier from the south bank of the Chippawa, about three and a half hours had elapsed. The battle of Chippawa had been short but bloody – according to the official returns, over seven hundred men were killed or wounded in the fields and woods around Street's Pine Grove farm.

The official British return, appended to Riall's report of the battle to his superior, Lieutenant General Gordon Drummond, dated 6 July 1814, lists a total of 485 casualties (148 killed, 321 wounded and 46 missing), broken down by unit as follows:[1]

Unit	Dead	Wounded	Missing
General Staff	-	1	-
Royal Artillery and RA Drivers	1	5	-
19th Light Dragoons	-	6	-
1st Foot	63	135	30
8th Foot	3	24	-
100th Foot	69	134	1
2nd Regiment, Lincoln Militia	12	16	15
Totals	148	321	46

Not surprisingly, the 1st and 100th Foot suffered worst, losing nearly half the numbers they had taken into action. The losses of the 2nd Lincolns were also bad and represented the highest casualty rate suffered by a Canadian sedentary militia unit in a single engagement during the war.

Riall provided no figure for the losses of the British native warriors, but an American estimate of British casualties suffered gives a figure of 87 warriors that, supposedly, would be based on an actual body count. This figure, however, is almost certainly too high and the Americans may have confused their own dead warriors with those of their enemy.[2]

The official American return, appended to Brown's report on the battle to Secretary of War John Armstrong dated 7 July 1814, provides a total of 278 casualties (58 dead, 241 wounded, and 19 missing) broken down as follows:[3]

Unit	Dead	Wounded	Missing
Scott's First Brigade			
Ninth Infantry	13	49	-
Eleventh Infantry	15	60	-
Twenty-Second Infantry	8	46	-
Twenty-Fifth Infantry	5	61	-
Ripley's Second Brigade			
Nineteenth Infantry	1	2	2
Twenty-Third Infantry	-	1	-
Porter's Third Brigade			
Fenton's Pennsylvania Regiment	3	2	7
Native warriors	9	4	10
Hindman's Artillery Battalion	4	16	-
Totals	58	241	19

According to this return, Brown lost about one sixth to one seventh of the men he took into action.

These "official" figures, compiled shortly after the battle was fought, have generally been accepted by historians. Recent research into military records in archives in London, Ottawa, and Washington has demonstrated, however, that the numbers of the dead contained in the official returns, especially the British return, are too high. The results of this research, with the number and names of the men killed on both sides, is contained in the appendices. Neither Brown or Riall misled their superiors by inflating their figures – their statistics were accurate given the context in which they were compiled and the vagaries of period record keeping. The variance is due to the fact that the "official" returns were compiled shortly after the battle ended and included in their numbers of dead many men who were actually prisoners. Based on this new research, the number of men killed on both sides (exclusive of those who died of wounds after the battle) from all nations was about two hundred.[4]

No method of casualty accounting, no matter how accurate, can convey the real cost of the battle, a price obvious to the Left Division as it marched back to its camp in the evening of 5 July. On the plain and in the woods around it lay hundreds of wounded, dying, and dead men sprawled where they had fallen. Stretcher parties were organized to bring in the wounded of both sides and the Usshers' house was turned into an emergency dressing station. But darkness had fallen before most of the casualties had been collected, and Captain Benjamin Ropes, who returned with his picket to the area of the farm buildings after the battle, recalled that many of the wounded lying scattered on Street's farm "died that Night & the groans of the Living was Shocking."[5]

There were fewer than twenty surgeons, surgeons' mates, and hospital stewards in the Left Division on 5 July. Overwhelmed by the sheer numbers of wounded, they worked without pause. Ropes, going into the farmhouse during the night, remembered that "their was not a room ... but what they had a man on the Table amphetating."[6] The medical personnel could not keep up – the wounded who had been brought in were still waiting for treatment when Ropes was relieved at 3 p.m. on 6 July, having been thirty-five hours on duty. Captain Joseph Henderson of the Twenty-Second, a doctor in civilian life, personally attended to his own casualties using a medical kit he had brought on campaign.[7]

Conditions were as bad in Chippawa. Captain Hamilton Merritt, arriving in the village with his troop of militia cavalry shortly after the battle ended, found that "every house" was "filled with the wounded." His men were forced to sleep under the sky, but Merritt managed to find a space inside one of the houses although he "spent a very unpleasant night" listening to the wounded in the neighbouring rooms "groaning with pain."[8]

As soon as possible, those British wounded who could make the eighteen-mile journey were transported to Fort George in unsprung supply wagons. Private Ferguson, who had obtained permission to visit his family at Christian Warner's in Stamford, arrived there at midnight on the day of the battle. His appearance was such that his wife and child "were much alarmed at first, seeing me in that state, but we had reason for thankfulness." In pain from his wound, Ferguson reported next day to the hospital at Fort George where he "found the scene most distressing" as "It was painful to witness the distress and agony of the wounded" having "their legs or arms amputated, some balls extracted from their wounds, and others, splinters of bones." A few days later, along with many of the British wounded, Ferguson was taken by boat to York and placed in a makeshift hospital.[9]

When dawn came on 6 July, the Left Division finished collecting the wounded and commenced the task of burying the dead of both sides. The greater number of corpses lay on the plain and these were almost certainly interred in shallow mass graves dug close to where they had fallen. The American burial parties were intrigued to find that the dead of the 1st Foot had fine brass belt plates engraved with a Sphinx and the word "Egypt" to commemorate that regiment's service there in 1802. These attractive items probably became souvenirs and were not turned in, as ordered, with the rest of the arms and equipment lying on the field. Detachments collected the corpses in the pine woods, and the dead were transported by wagon to the plain to be buried. The work of "cleaning up the battlefield," a grim and laborious, but necessary task, occupied the division throughout the day. It was not made any easier by the fact that 6 July proved to be another hot, humid day and the corpses were soon covered with myriads of flies.[10]

During the day, Riall sent a messenger under a flag of truce to Brown with an appeal "for the bodies of the officers killed, particularly for the militia; as it would be a great satisfaction for the relatives of the deceased to have them properly interred."[11] Brown refused this request, and according to Captain Samuel White, now a prisoner in Chippawa, the rumour in the British camp was that the American general had told the messenger "that he was able to bury all the dead he could kill."[12]

In contrast to their white counterparts, the American native warriors had a different attitude toward the dead and wounded of their enemy. Porter's warriors had suffered casualties in the woods and, according to their beliefs, they had to avenge these deaths. The best way to achieve this was by either taking prisoners to replace the men lost in battle or by taking their dead opponents' scalps. By their lights, the warriors saw no need to succour wounded enemies who had no value as prisoners, and these they put to death. These practises, which made perfectly good sense to the warriors, shocked their white allies.[13]

Early in the morning of 6 July, a deputation of twenty chiefs waited on Porter, each accompanied by a warrior bearing British scalps "strung on a stick and curved in the shape of a hoop, which had been taken on the previous day." The chiefs' purpose was twofold: to demonstrate to the American general the prowess of their men and to ask for a bounty for each scalp which they had heard would be paid by the American government. Angered, Porter "refused to examine or count these unseemly trophies, and ordered them to be buried or thrown into the river, which was immediately done."

Further differences between the two modes of warfare were brought home to the militia general later in the day, when he learned that his warriors had cut the throats of two wounded British warriors they had discovered in the woods. Porter remonstrated with them that "the act of taking the life of an unresisting man" was "cowardly and unworthy of a warrior" only to receive the bluntly honest reply that "it seemed very hard to put these men to death, but we hope you will consider that these are very bad times."[14]

While the Left Division cleaned up the battlefield, Riall composed his official report to his superior, Lieutenant General Gordon Drummond, on an action that was "not attended with the success which I had hoped for." Covering the events of three days, the British general managed to reduce the fighting both in the wood and on the plain to one paragraph:

> Our Indians and militia were shortly engaged with the enemy's riflemen and Indians, who at first checked their advance, but the light troops being brought to their support they succeeded after a sharp contest in dislodging them in a very handsome style. I placed two light 24 pounders and a 5 1/2 inch howitzer against the right of the enemy's position and formed the Royal Scots and 100th Regiment with the intention of making a movement on his left, which deployed with the greatest regularity and opened a heavy fire. I immediately moved up the King's Regiment to the right while the 100th and Royal Scots were directed to charge the enemy in front, for which they advanced with the greatest gallantry under fire. I am sorry to say, however, that in this attempt they suffered so severely that I was obliged to withdraw them, finding further efforts against the superior numbers of the enemy would be unavailing.[15]

Although he paid credit to the quality of his opponents, Riall attributed his defeat to the disparity between the forces, reporting that Brown had about six thousand men while he brought no more than eighteen hundred troops of all types into action. He informed Drummond that, from prisoners taken during the action, he had learned that Fort Erie had fallen and that Brown had been reinforced shortly before the battle had commenced.

Drummond accepted Riall's premise for his defeat, reporting up the chain of command to Lieutenant General Sir George Prevost that "nothing but the exceeding unequal numbers of the enemy could have prevented the attack from being covered with complete success."[16] The commander-in-chief was a bit more balanced – he concluded that the battle had "terminated less successfully than we have been accustomed to" because of the "improvement in discipline and the increased experience of the Enemy" who "evinced judgement in the position selected" and "had confidence in their numbers for its defence."[17] This was for public consumption – in private, Prevost had other ideas. To Major General George Glasgow, the Royal Artillery commander in North America, he confessed that, concerning the battle of Chippawa, "neither the Union of Science, organization or force will give the affair any éclat."[18]

As the victor, Brown had a much easier task and his official report, dated 7 July, is lengthier and more detailed than Riall's effort. Brown heaped generous praise on his subordinates, especially Scott whom Brown thought "entitled to the highest praises our country can bestow; to him more than any other man am I indebted for the victory" – which was no more than the truth.[19] Junior members of the division expressed it more simply. "Thus you will perceive that in a fair field fight we have flogged nearly double our Number of the Enemies choicest troops," wrote Captain George Howard of the Twenty-Fifth Infantry, "hurrah for Scott's Brigade!"[20]

There was no doubt in the Right Division that Chippawa had been a major defeat, and understandably, their morale was low. Norton remembered that the "Loss of our friends gave us all a gloomy appearance" and "in ev'ry division they seemed to think that they alone had more particularly fallen a sacrifice to the misfortune of the Day."[21] Picking up the theme of superior American numbers, many thought Riall should have refrained from attacking until after he had received reinforcements. It was "a British action," remarked Sergeant James Commins of the 8th Foot, but fought "against nearly six times our number."[22] Although he did not fight in the battle, Hamilton Merritt, who arrived at Chippawa shortly after its conclusion, must have discussed the battle with those who participated. "We candidly confessed we were beaten," he later wrote, "without prevarication."[23] Acknowledging that it was "a very delicate thing to censure a commanding officer," the Canadian was critical of Riall whom he believed

> acted hastily, neither did he employ all the means in his power. He sent away the 1st regiment of militia in the morning ... the 103rd were laying at Burlington, 800 strong, which could have been down in two days. There were, likewise, all the militia of the country, which, when assembled, would have ensured success. Had they attacked

us in the entrenchments, they would have fought to a very
great disadvantage.[24]

In sum, the prevailing feeling in the Right Division was that Chippawa was
not so much an American victory as a British defeat.

Are these criticisms valid? Was the Right Division defeated because of
the wrong decision on the part of its commander to attack a superior force?
To answer these questions, we have to examine the circumstances surrounding Riall's decision to attack, the intelligence he possessed that influenced
this decision, and his tactical handling of the battle.

On the morning of 5 July, having no information to the contrary, Riall
still believed that Fort Erie was holding out. He therefore assumed that a
large part of Brown's army was engaged in besieging that place, and according to his scouts, the American force camped south of Street's Creek
amounted to no more than two thousand men. As Riall possessed a force of
1360 regular infantry, 8 field pieces, as well as 200 militia and 300 warriors,
the odds were not bad. It was true that, given his strong position on the
north bank of the Chippawa, he had little to fear from the Americans, but
if Fort Erie fell the enemy before him would increase in strength. The
British general was confident that, given the superior quality of his troops
and the inconsistent performance of his opponents up to that time, he had
a reasonable chance of beating a slightly stronger American force. On the
basis of the information he possessed and on the operational situation,
Riall's decision to attack is defensible.

His first mistake, as Lieutenant Colonel George Hay noted, was that he
did not allow enough time for his light troops to clear completely the western woods of the enemy before advancing onto the plain. It might have
been better if the British general had waited while his light infantry and
native detachments secured this vulnerable flank. This, however, was not a
major error as the battle would be decided by the infantry and artillery
action on the plain – if Riall had won that action, American snipers in the
woods would have made little difference to the outcome.

Riall followed standard period British tactical doctrine of an artillery
bombardment followed by an attack in line, and left the tactical handling of
the battle to subordinates, whose work also cannot be faulted. Although it
was more usual for British regulars to stand first on the defensive, utilizing
their disciplined fire power to inflict casualties on an attacking enemy, Riall
chose to attack from the outset. This was an unusual decision but not an
incorrect one given the information he possessed about his enemy.

Riall and many of his subordinates chose to blame superior numbers
for the resulting defeat, but this claim does not bear close scrutiny. While it

is true that Brown's division outnumbered Riall's, much of it never saw action during the battle. The fight on the plain, the most important part of the action, reduces to approximately twelve hundred British regular infantry with six artillery pieces against approximately thirteen hundred and fifty American regular infantry with seven artillery pieces.

The Right Division lost that fight because, for the first time during the War of 1812, they encountered American troops who were their equal in training, motivation, and leadership. The First Brigade's musketry was as good as British regulars in regard to fire discipline and rate of fire, and perhaps marginally superior in terms of accuracy. The Americans deployed under fire as steadily as their opponents and there can be no doubt about their resolve – they stood up to the worst the Right Division had to offer without breaking. Finally, Scott's ability to recognize the opportunities that presented themselves allowed him to deploy in a tactical position that increased his firepower. In sum, Chippawa was indeed a "fair field fight" – and the British lost.

Riall's major error on 5 July 1814 was to underestimate the fighting qualities of the American regular soldier. Neither he nor his successors would repeat that mistake in the future.

"X-Ray" Photograph of U.S. Musket with "Buck and Ball" Round
This interesting photograph shows the interior of an American musket found in the 1970s near the site of the 1813 battle of Chateauguay in Lower Canada. Thrown away during the American retreat, it is still loaded with "buck and ball" (a musket ball and three buck shot). Used extensively by U.S. troops during the war, this type of projectile inflicted far less serious wounds than the normal musket ball.
Courtesy Parks Canada

W. Hamilton Merritt (1793-1862) in Old Age
As a twenty-one-year-old Canadian militia cavalry officer, Merritt arrived in Chippawa with his troop on the evening of the battle. He found "every house ... filled with wounded" and spent an "unpleasant night" kept awake by men "groaning with pain." Merritt was captured at Lundy's Lane but went on to postwar fame as the builder of the Welland Canal linking Lakes Ontario and Erie. Despite his distinguished war service, he bore no grudges against his former enemies and married an American woman.
Courtesy National Archives of Canada, C-29891

The Face of War – Sabre Wound
A gruesome portrait of a soldier, sketched by Surgeon Bell of the British army in a military hospital after the battle of Waterloo in 1815. The sketch shows the effect of a sabre cut to the head. War in 1814 was the same brutal business of hot- and cold-blooded killing as it is today.
Courtesy Parks Canada

The Face of War – The Effect of Round Shot on Human Beings
Round shot, the proverbial "cannon ball," was used to destroy structures and kill men and horses. Under optimum conditions, a 6-pdr. shot could penetrate nineteen men or seven feet of compacted earth. The result is shown here. Sketch by Surgeon Bell, 1815.
Courtesy Parks Canada

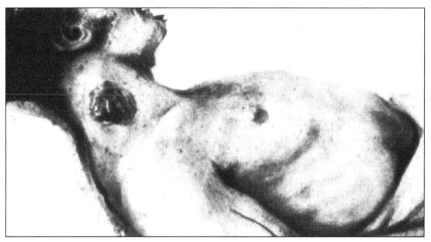

The Face of War – Canister Wound
This sketch shows the effect of an anti-personnel round fired by artillery.
Canister was a tin container filled with large lead bullets that disintegrated as it
left the muzzle of a gun, producing a deadly effect against dense formations of
infantry. Sketch by Surgeon Bell, 1815.
Courtesy Parks Canada

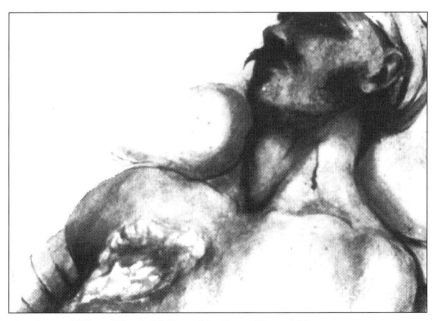

The Face of War – Wound Inflicted by Spent Round Shot
As evidenced by this man's caved-in chest, even spent round shot had a devas-
tating effect. Despite the elaborate uniforms and stately manoeuvring, warfare
in 1814 was a deadly business. Sketch by Surgeon Bell, 1815.
Courtesy Parks Canada

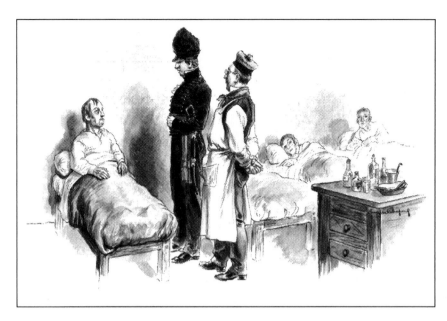

British Military Hospital During the War of 1812
Most hospitals after a battle were neither as comfortable nor as well appointed
as the one portrayed in this drawing. Private George Ferguson of the 100th
Foot, wounded at Chippawa, convalesced for weeks on the floor of a hastily
converted church in York. This was not made better by the fact that Ferguson, a
devout Methodist, was forced to listen to lengthy sermons by Bishop John
Strachan of York, a devout Anglican (Episcopalian).
Painting by Eugene Leliepvre, courtesy Parks Canada

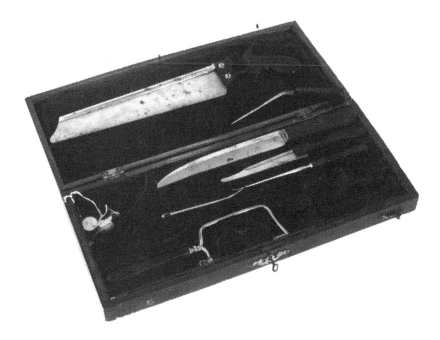

Surgeon's Amputation Kit, War of 1812

Amputation was the quickest and safest way to treat complicated wounds of the limbs and field surgeons excelled at it – with trained assistants and no undue complications, they could have a man's leg off above the knee in less than ten minutes. Captain Benjamin Ropes of the Twenty-First Infantry remembered visiting the Ussher farmhouse after the battle to find every room was filled with surgical teams performing amputations.

Courtesy Parks Canada

CHAPTER 11

THE LONG AND BLOODY
SUMMER OF 1814

For three days after the battle, the two armies stared at each other across the Chippawa. Then a local inhabitant told Brown of an abandoned logging trail that led from Street's farm to the bank of the Chippawa River near its junction with Lyon's Creek. On 8 July, the American commander sent half of his troops along this route with a bridging train while the other half kept Riall occupied by demonstrating in front of Chippawa village. Under fire, the Americans got their bridge about halfway across the river before Riall, deciding his position had become untenable, withdrew to Fort George.[1]

Leaving Porter's brigade to repair the Chippawa bridge, Brown pushed forward to Queenston, where from the Heights he expected to see the sails of Commodore Isaac Chauncey's squadron on Lake Ontario, seven miles distant. But there was no sign of the American navy. The Left Division sat at Queenston waiting for Chauncey for nearly two weeks.

This period was not without incident. Riall surrounded Brown's camp with a loose screen of Canadian militia and they proved very effective at reporting the movement of American patrols and ambushing small parties. On 12 July, the British commander left a strong garrison in the forts at the mouth of the Niagara River and withdrew the remainder of the Right Division west to the Twenty-Mile Creek. Brown now had a problem — should he move against the forts with the threat of a British army in his rear, or should he leave the forts in his rear and try to bring the British field force to battle? He pondered this question for several days, but on 20 July, he marched the division forward to Fort George, where he spent two days trying to lure the British garrison out to fight. When they did not budge, Brown was stuck. The heavy guns he needed for a formal siege were at Sackets Harbor and would have to be transported by Chauncey's squadron — but there was no sign of the commodore. Frustrated, Brown retraced his steps to Queenston on 23 July.

He decided to pursue Riall and force a fight, but first he wanted to lighten and re-supply his division. On 24 July, therefore, he sent his camp followers, baggage, and tents across the Niagara to Lewiston and then withdrew to Chippawa. This movement was made because, since it had first occupied the Pine Grove farm on 4 July, the division had been using Street's wharf as the terminus for boat traffic to and from Buffalo.

The American withdrawal surprised both Riall and Lieutenant General Gordon Drummond, who arrived early on 25 July to assume command in the Niagara peninsula. Throughout that day, both divisions made a series of moves and countermoves that brought them, at sunset into contact near the sand hill overlooking the junction of Lundy's Lane and the portage road. What followed was the hardest-fought engagement of the War of 1812, as both armies fed reinforcements into a confusing nighttime battle. Much of the fighting took place on land owned by the men of Captain John Rowe's company of the 2nd Lincolns, so badly cut up at Chippawa.

Both armies suffered heavy losses at the battle of Lundy's Lane. The official casualty figures were 878 British and Canadians and 860 American soldiers. Among the casualties were Drummond, Brown, and Scott who were wounded, and Riall, who was wounded and captured. Although the Left Division has a good claim to a tactical victory in the fighting; when it ended, they withdrew to their camp at Chippawa. Drummond, on the other hand, pulled the Right Division back to Queenston.

On 26 July, Ripley, who had assumed command of the American force, decided to retreat in the direction of Fort Erie. Before he did so, he ordered the burning of Bridgewater Mills, a little hamlet between Chippawa and the falls of Niagara, as well as the bridge over the Chippawa and the buildings of the Grove Farm. The Left Division arrived at Fort Erie the same day without incident and began to entrench.

Drummond gave the Americans a week of grace before he mounted a pursuit and they took full advantage of it, working by day and night to strengthen their position. After an attempt to lever the Left Division out of its position (by attacking its supply depots at Black Rock and Buffalo) came to grief at the battle of Conjocta Creek on 3 August, Drummond reluctantly undertook a siege. Everything was lacking – heavy guns, skilled engineers, tools, and supplies – and to make matters worse it rained almost daily for the next six weeks. After a desultory two day bombardment failed to affect the American position, Drummond mounted an assault on the night of 14 August. It was a costly disaster – the official figures were 905 British casualties and 62 American. Drummond continued the siege but was increasingly pessimistic about its outcome.

Elsewhere, the war was not going well for the United States. Peace negotiations had gotten underway at Ghent, Belgium, but the British delegates, sensing the tide had turned in their favour, presented stiff demands to their American counterparts. In early August, a small British force arrived in the Chesapeake and, after brushing aside a larger American army, captured Washington. Later though, it was rebuffed in an attempt to take Baltimore. At the same time, Prevost, the senior British general in North America, led a force of 10,000 veterans south from Montreal toward Plattsburg, New York. He encountered no resistance on his march because the American commander in that area, Major General George Izard, had been ordered to take his army west to the Niagara Peninsula.

In the meantime, the siege (really a blockade) of Fort Erie continued, but Drummond, feeling unable to afford the losses that such an attack would cost him, was reluctant to mount another assault. There was continuous skirmishing around the fort throughout this period, and on 5 September some British or Canadian marksman killed Joseph Willcocks. On 16 September, Drummond ordered an end to the siege and prepared to withdraw to Chippawa. On 17 September his engineers had just begun to remove the heavy guns from the seige emplacements when the Left Division sortied from the fort and attacked. This action resulted in 516 British casualties and 511 American casualties. A few days later, the British were behind the Chippawa River – the same position they had occupied on 5 July.

Meanwhile Prevost had not profited from Izard's absence from the Champlain valley. Arriving at Plattsburg on 6 September, he harried his naval commander into making a premature attack on the American squadron on Lake Champlain. The result was the loss of most of the British vessels, and a disheartened Prevost ordered a retreat to Canada.

Before Brown, who had rejoined the Left Division, could pursue the retreating British, he was joined by Izard's American Right Division. Being senior to Brown, Izard assumed command in the Niagara region and moved north to the Chippawa on 14 October. There he tried to lure Drummond out of his entrenchments on the north side of the river. Drummond refused to budge; he could afford to wait as the British fleet now controlled Lake Ontario. After a half-hearted flanking attempt was checked at the battle of Cook's Mills on 19 October, Izard withdrew south to Fort Erie. With winter coming on he wanted to get proper quarters for his troops – none could be found on the Canadian side – he decided to cross the Niagara to the United States. On 5 November, his engineers destroyed the entrenchments at the fort and the last American soldiers withdrew from Canadian soil.

The British reverses at Plattsburg and Baltimore softened the stance of their negotiators, and the peace talks made good progress. On Christmas

Eve, 1814, both nations signed the Treaty of Ghent agreeing on the pre-war *status quo,* and after thirty months of war, peace returned to North America.

It also returned to the Niagara but it was a cruel irony of the war that this happy and scenic region, far removed from the origins of the conflict, suffered some of the war's worst depredations. On the Canadian side, Newark, St. David's, and Bridgewater Mills were charred remnants while Queenston and Chippawa were only slightly more intact. On the American side, Youngstown, Lewiston, and Black Rock were largely destroyed while Buffalo, once a thriving village, was now a collection of quickly-built frame shacks surrounded by ruins. Both sides of the river presented a desolate landscape of burned-out and abandoned farms, torn-down fences, trampled crops, missing bridges, and hastily dug graves. It took a decade of hard work to undo the physical damage of the war – it took much longer to erase its memory in the minds of the survivors.

The Battle of Lundy's Lane, 25 July 1814
This engraving by William Strickland, first published in the *Portfolio* magazine in 1815, shows the central event of the bloody battle of Lundy's Lane fought three weeks after Chippawa – the capture of the British artillery by the Twenty-First Infantry. In a brutal slogging match that lasted nearly five hours and continued into the dark, Brown's Left Division and the British army fought each other to a standstill. Of the six generals present at the battle, five were wounded.
Courtesy National Archives of Canada, C-40721

Cemetery and Church at Lundy's Lane, 1860
The cemetery on top of the present-day Drummond Hill in the modern city of Niagara Falls, Canada, was the scene of the heaviest fighting during the battle of Lundy's Lane, 25 July 1814.
From Benson Lossing, *Pictorial Field Book of the War of 1812*, New York, 1869

Battle of Lundy's Lane, 25 July 1814
This dramatic but inaccurate nineteenth-century engraving portrays the
Twenty-First Infantry attacking the British artillery during the battle of Lundy's
Lane, 25 July 1814. More than 1600 American, British, and Canadian soldiers
were killed or wounded in this, the bloodiest battle of the War of 1812.
Courtesy National Archives of Canada, C-12094

**Major General George Izard,
U.S. Army (1776-1828)**
A product of military schools in
France, Germany, and England, Izard
was one of the best-trained officers
in the American army during the
war. In late September 1814, he
assumed command in the Niagara
area but, unable to make any head-
way, withdrew to the United States
in early November, bringing the
campaign to a close.
From Benson Lossing, *Pictorial Field Book of the
War of 1812*, New York, 1869

Congressional Medal Awarded to Jacob Brown, 1814

In November 1814 the U.S. Congress voted to award medals to the senior officers of the Left Division for their services in the Niagara campaign of 1814. This is a facsimile of the medal awarded to Jacob Brown.

From Benson Lossing, *Pictorial Field Book of the War of 1812*, New York, 1869

Congressional Medal Awarded to Winfield Scott, 1814

From Benson Lossing, *Pictorial Field Book of the War of 1812*, New York, 1869

Congressional Medal Awarded to Eleazar Ripley, 1814
From Benson Lossing, *Pictorial Field Book of the War of 1812*, New York, 1869

North East Demi-Bastion, Fort Erie, Canada
In the early hours of 15 August 1814, a British assault force took this bastion by a bayonet assault but were unable to penetrate further into the fort and capture the stone mess building, whose roof is seen in this photograph. During the fighting a magazine under the floor of the bastion was ignited and hundreds of men were killed in the ensuing confusion. Only at New Orleans in January 1815 did the British army suffer worse casualties during the war.

Photograph by Paul Kelly, courtesy *Canadian Military History* journal

Interior of Fort Erie, Canada
On 15 August 1814 a British force captured the bastion shown in the background but were unable to take the stone building on the right. Vicious close quarter fighting ensued in the narrow passageway between the bastion and the building as the British tried to get further into the fort and the Americans tried to retake the bastion.
Photograph by Paul Kelly, courtesy *Canadian Military History* journal

Commodore Isaac Chauncey,
U.S. Navy (1773-1840)
The senior American naval officer on the Great Lakes during the war, Chauncey was an intelligent and efficient administrator but a somewhat cautious commander. His full co-operation was a necessary precondition for the success of the seventh American invasion of Upper Canada in July 1814.
Courtesy National Archives of Canada,
C-010926

THE FATE OF THE BATTLEFIELD, 1814 - 1993

Samuel Street died in 1815 and did not live to see Pine Grove Farm restored to its prewar glory, although his estate was awarded £1333 for his war losses. The property passed to his daughter Mary, and eventually to her son Edgeworth Ussher, who constructed a new home called "Milford Lodge" very close to the location of the original house and barn occupied by Ropes's company on 5 July 1814. As a militia officer in 1837-38, Edgeworth Ussher was prominent in defending the frontier against the so-called "patriots" who were using the United States as a base to foment trouble on the Niagara peninsula. On the night of 16 November 1838 a gang of these thugs shot him dead as he went to answer the front door of his house.[1]

His widow, Sarah, continued to reside at Milford Lodge with her three children until 1857 when she sold the house and a sickle-shaped strip of the plain to William Gray. Sometime before 1876, a road was constructed west from the river road along the curved southern boundary of Gray's property. It became known as Edgeworth Road in honour of the murdered officer, while Street's Creek became known as Ussher's Creek. By this time, however, most of the original area of the Grove Farm had been sub-divided into smaller parcels, and no Streets or Usshers resided on them.

Throughout the next century, the battlefield changed hands many times, although it remained primarily agricultural land. Sometime during this period, a house and farm buildings were erected just north of Ussher's Creek and, in the 1920s, Milford Lodge was moved from its original location to the northwest corner of the junction of Edgeworth and the river roads. It was later demolished. In the 1950s, a small subdivision was built on the northern end of the plain facing the river road.

With the exception of these encroachments, however, the battlefield remains much the same at it was in 1814. The visitor can still make out the original tree line that marked the boundary of the swampy, obstructed western woods where Porter's men fought the 2nd Lincolns, British warriors, and light infantry. The infamous "strip of woodland" that divided the plain from the Chippawa River is there, albeit in abbreviated form, and the modern bridge over Street's (now Ussher's Creek) is located about where its 1814 predecessor stood. The house and barn where that notorious speller, Benjamin Ropes, sheltered his picket from the British sniping parties are gone, but the place where they stood can easily be identified. Chippawa is so intact that it does not take too much imagination to walk into that nondescript field today and visualize the events of 5 July 1814. Be careful – if you stand there long enough you will begin to hear the crackle of musketry and war whoops issuing from the woods to the west.

There is no monument on the site of the battle, although there is a small plaque on the wrong side of the river road giving the skeletal details of the action. To the casual visitor the battlefield today is an unremarkable flat farm field, but to the enlightened it is the final resting place of some two hundred American, British, and Canadian soldiers, and native warriors from many different nations.

Despite a local legend that Brown burned the British dead while transporting the bodies of his own men across the Niagara, the evidence is plentiful that the Left Division interred the dead of both armies on the plain. They were still there when the British re-occupied the area a few weeks later – on 30 July 1814. Lieutenant Joseph Mermet of De Watteville's Regiment visited the site and wrote to a friend that: "I saw the battlefield near Chippawa, it was strewn with the dead of the enemy."[2] Mermet, a very literary man judging by his correspondence, was speaking figuratively – what he meant was that the plain "was strewn with the graves of the enemy." What he didn't realize was that most of those graves contained British soldiers and their allies.

The evidence is indisputable that the dead of the battle were buried on the plain and there is no evidence that they were dis-interred after the war and relocated. They have been there since 1814 although, as the ground has been almost continuously farmed in the intervening 180 years, they may not rest undisturbed. It matters not – for this ground is hallowed by their presence.[3]

Plaque for the Battle of Chippawa
The only memorial for the battle is this small plaque located on the river road
on the banks of the Niagara River. Some of the details in the inscription are
incorrect, not the least of which is the statement that the American army at the
battle was commanded by Winfield Scott. No mention is made of the fact that
the dead from both sides are buried not far from where this memorial is located.
The two flags placed at the memorial are a reminder that since 1815 the United
States and Canada have lived in peace as good neighbours.
Photograph by Robert Foley, 5 July 1993

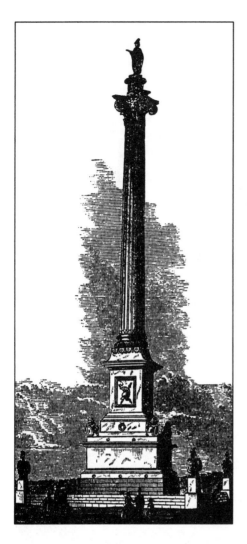

Brock's Monument, Queenston Heights, Canada

This imposing memorial, erected in the 1850s on the heights overlooking Queenston, contains the mortal remains of Major General Sir Isaac Brock and his aide, killed during the battle of Queenston Heights of 13 October 1812. Clearly visible from the U.S. side of the Niagara River, it serves as a reminder to Americans that Canada is a sovereign nation that fought a war to preserve its independence.

From Benson Lossing, *Pictorial Field Book of the War of 1812*, New York, 1869

Lundy's Lane Memorial, Drummond Hill, Niagara Falls, Canada
This memorial, which incorporates a mausoleum that holds some of the mortal remains of the British and Canadian dead of the battle, was erected in 1895. It is shown here decorated for the centenary of the battle in July 1914. Although nearly every other major action of the war fought in Canada is marked with a similar monument, the only memorial for Chippawa is a modest plaque containing a brief description of the action.

From *Centenary Celebration of the Battle of Lundy's Lane*, Niagara Falls, 1919, courtesy Lundy's Lane Historical Society

Appendices

APPENDIX A
Order of Battle,
Left Division, U.S. Army,
5 July 1814

Commanding Officer — Maj. Gen. Jacob Brown

Divisional Staff

Aides to Gen. Brown — Capt. Loring Austin
Capt. Ambrose Spencer

Adjutant General — Col. Charles K. Gardner
Assistant Adjutant General — Maj. Roger Jones
Chief Engineer — Lt. Col. William McRee
Assistant Engineer — Maj. Eleazar D. Wood
Quartermaster — Capt. John Camp
Acting Inspector General — 2nd Lt. Edward B. Randolph

First Brigade (1319)

Commanding Officer — Brig. Gen. Winfield Scott
Aide to Scott — 1st Lt. William Jenkins Worth
Brigade Major — Lt. J.D. Smith

Ninth/Twenty-Second
Infantry (549) — Maj. Henry Leavenworth
Eleventh Infantry (416) — Maj. John McNeil
Twenty-Fifth Infantry (354) — Maj. Thomas S. Jesup

Second Brigade (992)

Commanding Officer — Brig. Gen. Eleazar Ripley
Aide — 1st Lt. William MacDonald
Brigade Major — 1st Lt. Newman S. Clarke

Twenty-First Infantry (651) — Maj. Joseph Grafton
Twenty-Third Infantry (341) — Maj. Daniel McFarland

Note: Only Captain Benjamin Ropes's company of the Twenty-First Infantry was actively engaged during the action. The Twenty-First Infantry included an "orphan" company each of the Seventeenth and Nineteenth Infantry Regiments.

Third Brigade (926)

Commanding Officer	Brig. Gen. Peter B. Porter, New York Militia
Aide	Maj. Jacob Dox, New York Militia
Brigade Major	Maj. John Stanton, New York Militia
5th Pennsylvania Regiment (Fenton's Pennsylvanians) (540)	Maj. James Wood, Pennsylvania Militia
Native Warriors (386)	Lt. Col. Erastus Granger

Artillery (327)

Maj. Jacob Hindman's Battalion, Corps of Artillery

Capt. Thomas Biddle	est. 3 x 12-pdr. guns (80)
Capt. John Ritchie	2 x 6-pdr. guns, 1 x 5.5 in. howitzer (96)
Capt. Nathan Towson	2 x 6-pdr. guns, 1 x 5.5 in. howitzer (89)
Capt. Alexander Williams	est. 3 x 18-pdr. guns (62)
Artillery Reserve	(unknown numbers and calibres)

Note: Only Towson and Ritchie's companies, and one 12-pdr. gun of Biddle's company came into action on 5 July 1814.

Cavalry (70)

Capt. Samuel D. Harris's Company (Troop), U.S. Light Dragoons

Recapitulation of Number of U.S. Troops Present at Chippawa

	Present	*Engaged in Action*
First Brigade	1319	1319
Second Brigade	992	80*
Third Brigade	540	200
Native Warriors	386	300
Artillery:		
Towson's Company	89	89
Biddle's Company	80	25**
Ritchie's Company	96	96
Williams's Company	62	-
Totals	3564	2109

* Ropes's company of the Twenty-First Infantry
** As Biddle brought only one of his three guns into action, this is an
estimate.

Sources: Strength of the First, or Scott's Brigade, 30 June 1814 in Henry
Adams, *History*, IV, Book VIII, 35; Strength of the Second, or Ripley's
Brigade, 1 July 1814, Adams, *History*, IV, Book VIII, 36; Strength of
Hindman's Battalion of Artillery, 1 July 1814, Adams, *History*, IV, Book
VIII, 37; Strength of Major General Brown's Army, Buffalo, 1 July 1814,
Adams, *History*, IV, Book VIII, 37; "U.S. Unit Strength as Shown by
Ration Abstracts for the Months, July through September, 1814," con-
tained in Whitehorne, Fort Erie, Annex D, 115; Graves, *Lundy's Lane*,
Appendix A; Porter to Stone, 26 May 1840, *Doc. Hist.* II, 356; Cates,
"Ropes," 117.

APPENDIX B
Order of Battle
Right Division, British Army in Canada,
5 July 1814

Commanding Officer, Right Division Maj. Gen. Phineas Riall
Staff
 Aide to Maj. Gen. Riall   Capt. J.H. Holland

Infantry (1560)
 1st Foot (Royal Scots)(500) Lt. Col. John Gordon
 8th Foot (King's Regiment)(400) Maj. Thomas Evans
 100th Foot (460)   Lt. Col. George Hay, the
             Marquis of Tweeddale
 2nd Lincoln Regiment (Militia) Lt. Col. Thomas Dickson
  (200)

Artillery (est. 70)
 Capt. James Mackonochie's Brigade, Capt. James Maclachlane's
  Company, Royal Artillery
 Lt. Edmund Sheppard   3 x 6-pdr. field guns
 Lt. R.S. Armstrong   2 x 24-pdr. field guns
 Lt. T. Jack   1 x 5.5 in. howitzer

Cavalry (est. 70)
 Troop, 19th Light Dragoons Maj. Robert Lisle

Native Warriors (est. 300)
 Western nations (100)
 Grand River nations (200)

Recapitulation of Number of British Troops in Action at Chippawa

British Regulars	
Infantry	1360
Artillery	est. 70
Cavalry	est. 70
Canadian Militia	est. 200
Native Warriors	est. 300
Total	2000

Sources: Abstract of Weekly Distribution Return of the Right Division, 22 June 1814, Cruikshank, *Doc. Hist.*, I, 28; Riall to Drummond, 6 July 1814, NA, RG 8 I, vol. 684, 51; Drummond to Prevost, 10 July 1814, Cruikshank, *Doc. Hist.*, I, 35; Drummond to Prevost, 12 July 1814, Cruikshank, *Doc. Hist.*, I, 35; Merritt, *Journal,* 55-56.

APPENDIX C
Weapons and Weapons Performance at Chippawa, 5 July 1814

1. Infantry Weapons
    a. *British Short Land Musket, India Pattern*

Furniture	Brass
Calibre of bore	75 (.75 of an inch)
Projectile	Soft lead ball, weighing just over one ounce

Range	
Theoretical Maximum	250 yards
Effective Maximum	
Volley (100 rounds)	150 yards
Single round	100 yards
Favoured Range	50-75 yards
Weight	9.5 lbs. without bayonet
Optimum Effect at 30 Yards	Penetrate 3/8 inch of iron or 5 inches of seasoned oak

Rate of Fire by Trained Infantry	
Optimum	4-5 rounds per minute
Actual	2-3 rounds per minute
Rate of Misfire	20-40% depending on conditions

    b. *American 1795 Springfield, or Later Variants*

Furniture	Steel
Calibre of bore	.69
Projectile	Soft lead ball, weighing just under one ounce

Range	
Theoretical Maximum	less than 250 yards
Effective Maximum	
Volley (100 rounds)	less than 150 yards
Single round	less than 100 yards
Favoured Range	50-75 yards
Weight	11 lbs. with bayonet
Effect	Less than that of the British musket depending on the type of round used, (e.g. ball or buck and ball)
Rate of Fire and Misfire	Same as British weapon

Notes: Depending on quality of powder and flint, the touch-holes of these muskets had to be manually cleared every fifteen to twenty rounds and the flint replaced every ten to fifteen rounds. After fifteen repeated rounds the barrel became too hot to handle comfortably.

2. Artillery Weapons
   a. British
      i. Brass 24-pdr. gun:

Weight on Carriage	4963 lbs.
Number of Horses in Team	6-8
Service Life	500-600 rounds at service charge
Gun Detachment	
Trained Gunners	3
Assistants	5
Calibre	
Bore	5.8 in./148 mm
Projectile (Round Shot)	5.53 in.
Weight of Projectile (Round Shot)	24 lbs./52.8 kg
Range	
Round Shot	
Theoretical Maximum	2000 yds.
Effective Maximum	1000-1200 yds.
Favoured Range	800-1000 yds.
Canister	600 yds.
Effectiveness	Under optimum conditions, a 24-pdr. round shot could penetrate 40 human beings
Rate of Fire	One round per minute
Ammunition Scales	Probably 60-70 rounds, 75% round shot, with more in immediate supply

      ii. Brass 6-pdr. gun:

Weight of Gun, Carriage, and Limber	3080 lbs.
Number of Horses in Team	4-6
Service Life	500-600 rounds at service charge
Gun Detachment	
Trained Gunners	2-3
Assistants	3-4

Calibre
  Bore   3.66 in./83 mm
  Projectile (Round Shot)   3.49 in.
Weight of Projectile
  (Round Shot)   6 lbs./13.2 kg
Range
  Round Shot
    Theoretical Maximum   1000 yds.
    Effective Maximum   600-800 yds.
    Favoured Range   600-800 yds.
  Canister   200-600 yds.
  Effectiveness   Under optimum conditions, a 6-pdr. round shot could penetrate 19 human beings

Rate of Fire   1-2 rounds per minute
Ammunition Scales   40 round shot and 10 rounds of canister with the gun and limber. The ammunition carriage contained 92 round shot, 18 canister, and 20 shrapnel rounds

iii. Brass 5.5 inch howitzer:
    Weight of Howitzer
      (Carriage and Limber)   3052 lbs.
    Number of Horses in Team   4-6
    Service Life   500-600 rounds at service charge
    Gun Detachment
      Trained Gunners   2-3
      Assistants   3-4
      Calibre of bore   5.5 in./139.7 mm
    Range
      Theoretical Maximum   1000 yds.
      Effective Maximum   600-800 yds.
      Favoured Range   600-800 yds.
    Rate of Fire   1 round per minute
    Ammunition Scales   16 shells and 4 canister rounds with the howitzer and limber. A further 46 shells, 6 canister, and shrapnel carried with the ammunition wagon

b. American
 i. Iron 6-pdr. gun:

Weight of Gun and Carriage	2000 lbs.
Number of Horses in Team	4-6
Service Life	Estimated 1000 rounds at service charge
Gun Detachment	
Trained Gunners	3
Assistants	6
Calibre	
Bore	3.66 in./83 mm
Projectile (Round Shot)	3.49 in.
Weight of Projectile (Round Shot)	6 lbs./13.2 kg
Range and Effectiveness	See figures for British brass 6-pdr. gun
Rate of Fire	1-2 rounds per minute
Ammunition Scales	18 round shot on carriage and 62 round shot and 30 canister rounds in their caissons

 ii. Iron 5.5 inch howitzer:

Weight of Howitzer and Carriage	2100 lbs.
Number of Horses in Team	4-6
Service Life	Est. 1000 rounds at service charge
Gun Detachment	
Trained Gunners	2-3
Assistants	3-4
Calibre of bore	5.5 in./139.7 mm
Range, Effectiveness, Rate of Fire	Same as British 5.5 howitzer

Sources: Muskets: Howard Blackmore, *British Military Firearms, 1650-1850* (London, 1961); René Chartrand, *Uniforms and Equipment of the United States Forces in the War of 1812* (Youngstown, 1992); William Duane, *American Military Library* (Philadelphia, 1809) 2 vols.; William Greener, *The Gun; or, A Treatise on the Various Descriptions of Small Fire-Arms* (London, 1808); James Hicks, *Notes on U.S. Ordnance* (Mt. Vernon, 1940); and B.P. Hughes, *Firepower, Weapons Effectiveness on the Battlefield, 1630-1850* (London, 1974).

Artillery: Ralph W. Adye, *The Bombardier and Pocket Gunner* (London, 1813); Henri Othon De Scheel, *Treatise on Artillery* (Philadelphia, 1800);

Jean-Jacques Basiline de Gassendi, *Aide-Memoire, à l'usage des Officiers de l'artillerie de France* (Paris, 1801) 2 vols.; [Amos Stoddard], *Exercise for the Garrison and Field Ordnance, Together with Manoeuvres of Horse Artillery ...* (Philadelphia, 1812); and Louis de Tousard, *American Artillerist's Companion, or Elements of Artillery* (Philadelphia, 1809) 2 vols.

APPENDIX D
American Regulars, Militia, and Native Warriors Killed at Chippawa

List 1. REGULAR ARMY AND PENNSYLVANIA VOLUNTEERS

Name	*Rank*

Ninth United States Infantry Regiment

1.	McQuentin, Hugh	Sergeant
2.	Bradley, Asa	Private
3.	Churchill, Abisha[a]	Private
4.	Gates, Edmund	Private

Eleventh United States Infantry Regiment

1.	Belding, William	Corporal
2.	Latham, Simon	Corporal
3.	Simons, Elam	Corporal
4.	Tower, Horace B.	Corporal
5.	Avery, Shadrack	Private
6.	Brigham, Thomas	Private
7.	Fiske, Benjamin	Private
8.	Frimer, Nicholas	Private
9.	Jefts, Trainus	Private
10.	Marsell, Stephen	Private
11.	Merriam, William	Private
12.	Miles, Thomas	Private
13.	Prio, Joseph	Private
14.	Sprague, Frederick	Private
15.	Wheeler, Jacob	Private

Nineteenth United States Infantry Regiment (attached to Twenty-First Infantry)

1.	Mingro, Joseph	Private
2.	Mu ..., James[b]	Private
3.	Mullenic, Elijah	Private

Twenty-First United States Infantry Regiment

1.	Strong, John R.[c]	Private

Twenty-Second United States Infantry Regiment

1.	Kirk, John	Corporal
2.	Brown, Jeremiah	Private
3.	Coil, William	Private
4.	Cross, Anthony	Private
5.	Dixon, William	Private
6.	Dunmore, Daniel	Private
7.	Gould, Benjamin	Private
8.	Ord, John	Private
9.	Reed, Samuel	Private
10.	Rinehart, Jacob	Private
11.	Scroggs, Joseph	Private
12.	West, Thomas	Private
13.	Wright, John	Private

Twenty-Third United States Infantry Regiment

1.	Gould, John	Private

Twenty-Fifth United States Infantry Regiment

1.	_____ d	Sergeant
2.	Armstrong, Ho____ e	Private
3.	Blair, John	Private
4.	Bliss, Francis	Private
5.	Cairn, John O.	Private
6.	Crocker, Isaacf	Private
7.	Morris, Thomas	Private

Captain Nathan Towson's Company, Hindman's Battalion, U.S. Artillery

1.	Boyal, William	Private
2.	Steward, John	Private

Colonel Alexander Fenton's Regiment, 5 Pennsylvania Volunteers

1.	Bull, Robert	Lieutenant Colonel
2.	Bunker, John	Private
3.	Fry, Joseph	Private
4.	Hughes, John	Private
5.	Irwin, Johng	Private
6.	McClelland, Robert	Private
7.	Miller, James	Private

Numerical Totals

Number confirmed killed and probably buried at Chippawa 49
Others (died of wounds after battle, missing in action)
  who may or may not be buried at Chippawa 4
Total Americans who may be buried at Chippawa 53

Sources: United States National Archives: Record Group 94: Entry 55, Muster Rolls; Entry 71, Eaton's Compendium; Entry 407, Contractor's Accounts; Entry 510, Service Records; Record Group 98, Company Books.

This list was compiled by Lieutenant Colonel Joseph Whitehorne, U.S. Army (Retd.).

List 2. AMERICAN NATIVE WARRIORS

Name	*Nation (Tribe)*	*Rank*
1. Two Guns	Seneca	Warrior
2. Ga-nos-ea-ja-eot-gch	Seneca	Warrior
3. De-yi-goh-has-ha	Seneca	Warrior

To date, only these three names of the nine American native warriors known to have been killed at the battle have been confirmed. It is known that warriors of the Tuscarora, Oneida, and Cayuga nations took part in the battle.

Sources: U.S. National Archives, Bureau of Indian Affairs, New York Indian Agency, Letters Received, Reels 587 and 588. Information provided by Professors Howard Vernon and Lawrence Hauptman of State University of New York, New Paltz, NY.

[a] Private Abisha Churchill, 9th Infantry, died of wounds on 7 July 1814 and may have been buried at the military hospital in Williamsville, NY.

[b] This soldier's surname is illegible in the original records.

[c] Private John R. Strong, 21st Infantry, listed as missing in action 4 July 1814 and may not be buried at Chippawa.

[d] This sergeant's name is illegible in the original records.

[e] This soldier's Christian name is illegible in the original records.

[f] Private Isaac Crocker, 25th Infantry is listed as having died of wounds, 9 July 1814 and may be buried at the military hospital in Williamsville, NY.

[g] Private John Irwin of the Pennsylvania Volunteers is listed as missing in action and may not be buried at Chippawa.

APPENDIX E
British Regulars, Canadian Militia, and Native Warriors Killed at Chippawa

List 1. BRITISH OFFICERS

1.	Capt. [Percy] Bailly [Baillie]	1st Foot
2.	Lt. [Patrick] Gibbons	100th Foot
3.	Ensign [John] Rea	100th Foot

Sources: National Archives of Canada, Record Group 8 I, vol. 684, 55, "Return of the Killed, Wounded and Missing of the Right Division in Action with the Enemy in Advance of Chippawa, 5th July, 1814." Christian names and alternate spellings supplied from the *Army List, 1814.*

List 2. BRITISH ENLISTED PERSONNEL

Rank Abbreviations

Cpl.	Corporal
C/Sgt.	Colour Sergeant
Gnr.	Gunner
Pte.	Private
Sgt.	Sergeant

Name	Rank	Age	Place and County of Origin or Enlistment
Captain James MacLachlane's Company, Royal Artillery			
1. John Gauk (Gawke)	Gnr.	-	-
1st Battalion, 1st Regiment of Foot, The Royal Scots			
1. Hay Fenton	Sgt.	-	Army
2. John Pearson	Sgt.	37	Edinburgh, Midlothian
3. James Graham	Cpl.	-	Perthshire
4. John Burgess (Burges)	Pte.	-	Cheshire
5. James Campbell	Pte.	24	Dinigars, Antrim
6. John Carr	Pte.	25	Rosneath, Argyllshire
7. William Carroll	Pte.	27	Longford
8. Henry Chapman	Pte.	25	Wilham, Leicestershire

9.	Phillip Cooper	Pte.	-	-
10.	Hugh Corcoran	Pte.	-	-
11.	John Cox	Pte.	34	Lincolnshire
12.	Michael Devine	Pte.	36	Dunmore, Wicklow
13.	Peter Donaghey	Pte.	34	Torenskin, Tyrone
14.	William Donaghey	Pte.	27	Confeckle, Tyrone
15.	Jeremiah Foley	Pte.	31	Ireland
16.	Frederick Fry	Pte.	29	Winslough
17.	Richard Gallery	Pte.	30	Rathkeale, Limerick
18.	James Gay	Pte.	35	Ardtrea, Tyrone
19.	John Grubb	Pte.	32	Mimuir, Forfar
20.	David Gunn	Pte.	37	Dudeston, Midlothian
21.	James Harris	Pte.	22	Ottery, Devon
22.	Lawrence F. Healey	-	27	-
23.	John Hinch	Pte.	36	Coolgraney, Wexford
24.	George Jones	Pte.	21	England
25.	Thomas Kelly	Pte.	34	Longford
26.	Alexander Kennedy	Pte.	21	Kilfinnan, Limerick
27.	Bryan Lawen	Pte.	38	Calus, Tyrone
28.	Hugh Lungan	Pte.	32	Calus, Tyrone
29.	Thomas Monaghan	Pte.	40	Drumholm, Donegal
30.	Patrick McKindray	Pte.	19	Ireland
31.	Joseph McLean	Pte.	24	Baleron, Down
32.	Alexander McLough	Pte.	26	Aberdeedy, East Lothian
33.	William Neilson	Pte.	26	Bervie, Kincardineshire
34.	Henry Nugent	Pte.	30	Donegal, Donegal
35.	Henry Stanley	Pte.	-	-
36.	James Stewart	Pte.	26	-
37.	Thomas Sullivan	Pte.	22	Ireland
38.	Hugh Trower	Pte.	32	Drummoor, Donegal
39.	John Wanton	Pte.	29	-
40.	James West	Pte.	28	Camberwell, Surrey
41.	George Worthy	Pte.	-	England

1st Battalion, 8th Regiment of Foot, The King's Regiment

1.	James Dougherty	Pte.	-	-
2.	James Mahon	Pte.	-	Feverly, Rosscomm

100th Regiment of Foot, Prince Regent's County of Dublin Regiment

1.	Robert Armstrong	C/Sgt.	-	-
2.	John Glass	Sgt.	-	Leitrim
3.	John Havlin	Cpl.	-	-
4.	Michael Brown	Pte.	-	-
5.	James Burns	Pte.	-	-
6.	Gerrard Byrne	Pte.	-	Dublin
7.	James Carty	Pte.	-	-
8.	Bryan Cavanagh	Pte.	-	-
9.	John Cleary	Pte.	-	-
10.	Thomas Crawford	Pte.	-	-
11.	James Cullen	Pte.	-	-
12.	Peter Fagan	Pte.	-	-
13.	Cunningham Fleming	Pte.	-	Tyrone
14.	John Freeburn	Pte.	-	-
15.	James Gloarny (Glorney)	Pte.	-	-
16.	Christopher Guggerty	Pte.	-	-
17.	Richard Hanly	Pte.	-	-
18.	Edward Kelly	Pte.	-	-
19.	Michael Kelly	Pte.	-	-
20.	Darby King	Pte.	-	-
21.	Bernard McBride	Pte.	-	-
22.	John McIntire	Pte.	-	Derry
23.	Thomas McMahon	Pte.	-	-
24.	James Shields	Pte.	-	-
25.	James Traynor	Pte.	-	-
26.	James Trulock	Pte.	-	-
27.	Williams Williams	Pte.	-	-

Sources: Douglas L. Hendry, "British Casualties Suffered at Chippawa, 5 July, 1814," Directorate of History, DND. This report is based on War Office documents located in the Public Record Office, London.

List 3. CANADIAN MILITIA

2nd Lincoln Regiment

1.	Captain John Rowe [Row]

2.   Captain George Turney [Turner]
3.   Lieutenant Christopher McDonald [McDonnel, McDonnell, McDouall]
4.   Volunteer John Hill
5.   James Forsyth [Forsythe]
6.   Sergeant John Thompson
7.   Private Samuel Adams
8.   Private Joseph Bastide [Bastido, Bastedo, Baslider]
9.   Private Lewis Blanshet [Blanchette, Blanchell]
10.   Private Thomas Bloomfield [Blumfield]
11.   Private John Thompson [Thomson]
12.   Private Stephen Peer
13.   Private Timothy Skinner
14.   Private Alexander McDonald [McDonell]
15.   Private Stephen Peer
16.   Private Timothy Skinner
17.   Private Robert Taylor [Teelor]
18.   Private Sergeant John Hutt
19.   Private Jacob Wilkinson

Other Militia Units

Sergeant Henry Eberts, Western Rangers (Caldwell's Rangers)
Private Pierre Beauchamp, Lytle's Rangers (The Loyal Essex)

Sources: National Archives of Canada, Record Group 9, I B 4, vol. 1, 98-99, "A Return of the Militia Men who were Killed and Wounded in the Sortie which took place on the 5th instant from the Lines of Chippawa," 6 July 1814; and notes from William Gray of Toronto.

Only the names of those known to have been killed at Chippawa have been included, the names of the wounded have been excluded. As some of the above men may have been wounded in the action but taken back to the British line for treatment only to later die of their wounds, they may not be buried on the ground.

Period spelling was extremely variable. The alternate spellings enclosed in square brackets were extracted from: National Archives of Canada, Record Group 9, I B 1, File "Lincoln Militia, 1816," "Pension List of 2nd Lincoln Regiment for Persons Killed in Action with the Enemy, 11 July, 1816"; a list of widows and orphans for militiamen killed in action contained in the *Niagara Spectator*, 25 October 1816; and notes from William Gray of Toronto.

List 4. British Native Warriors

	Name	Nation (Tribe)	Rank	Widow(s)
1.	Big Horn	Delaware	War Chief	1
2.	Thinyawegh's brother	Cayuga	Chief	-
3.	[not named]*	Cherokee	Warrior	-
4.	Tchuchichea's cousin*	Cherokee	Warrior	-
5.	Kellaawee	Chippawa	Warrior	-
6.	Kennewasabic	Chippawa	Warrior	-
7.	Maader	Chippawa	Warrior	-
8.	Mishanoquis	Chippawa	Warrior	1
9.	Missquenini	Chippawa	Warrior	1
10.	Mussasska's son	Chippawa	Warrior	-
11.	Muswaga	Chippawa	Warrior	-
12.	Pandaequawy	Chippawa	Warrior	2
13.	Obohidia	Delaware	Warrior	1
14.	Abeanetong	Delaware	Warrior	1
15.	Sastrahuseo	Huron	Warrior	1
16.	Young Wood	Sauk	Warrior	1

* The unnamed Cherokee warrior and the warrior identified as Tchuchichea's cousin may be one and the same, this is not clear from the documents. In addition, in his letter dated 26 October 1814, Norton states that warriors of the Muncey and Moravian nations were killed at the battle but gives no further details.

Notes: The names have been transcribed as they appeared in the documents but British orthography of Indian names during this period was extremely variable and the names in the above list are at best a phonetic approximation of the native original.

Sources: National Archives of Canada: Record Group 10: volume 3, p. 1546, Norton to McMahon, 26 October 1814; volume 12, p. 1052, "Return of Indians killed in the Service between the 1st Sep. 1813 and 1st Sep. 1814"; Record Group 8 I, volume 261, Norton to Addison, 13 February 1817.

APPENDIX F
Myths and Anecdotes of the Battle of Chippawa

1. The Origins of the Grey Uniforms of the West Point Cadets

The uniforms of the corps of cadets of the U.S. Military Academy at West Point are grey as opposed to the more traditional blue of American army full dress. According to Scott, the origins of these grey uniforms derive from the grey jackets issued to his First Brigade at Buffalo in the spring of 1814. In 1864, he wrote that "In compliment to the battle of Chippewa, our military cadets have worn gray coats ever since."[1] Before his death in 1866, he explained to the historian, Benson Lossing, that "in honor of Scott and his troops, that style of cloth was adopted at the Military Academy at West Point as the uniform of the cadets" and "has been used ever since."[2]

It would be nice if this was true, but apparently the cadets at West Point began wearing grey as early as the summer of 1814 for a more prosaic reason – a shortage of blue cloth in the United States. In November 1815, the commandant of the academy reported to the secretary of war that the cadets had been wearing grey cloth since August 1814 and asked that it be adopted as the official uniform colour. His request was granted and the uniform of the cadets has been grey since that time.[3]

The origin of the cadets' grey uniforms does not matter, what is important is that they perpetuate the memory of the Left Division of the United States Army, an organization that deserves such remembrance.

2. The American Army Burned the British Dead After the Battle

From time to time, it has been asserted that the American army burned the British dead after the battle. The source of this myth (for that is what it is) can probably be traced to an early Canadian work, David Thompson's *History of the Late War between Great Britain and the United States of America*, published in Niagara-on-the-Lake in 1832. On page 227, Thompson, a veteran of the Royal Scots, states that the "Three or four days subsequent to the sanguinary conflict on the plains of Chippawa, were mostly employed by the enemy in burying their dead and burning those of the British."[4] Writing in 1896, local Canadian historian William Kirby embellished this theme:

> The enemy disgraced humanity after the battle. They buried their own dead on the field, but the bodies of the British soldiers and militiamen who had fallen were piled in heaps with layers of wood and fence rails and shamefully burnt on the field.[5]

Three weeks later, according to Kirby, after the battle of Lundy's Lane,

> the American dead were, in retaliation for the burning of
> our dead at Chippawa, piled in great funeral pyres with
> wood in heaps under them and burnt to ashes. It was a sad
> and sorrowful sight, but the conduct of the enemy at
> Chippawa compelled this act of retaliation.[6]

All of this is manifestly untrue. The evidence is overwhelming that the
Left Division buried the British dead after the battle of Chippawa.[7] It was
the British who, for reasons of expediency and sanitation, burned the
American dead after the battle of Lundy's Lane.[8]

3. Scott Nearly Captured on the Morning of the Battle

There is an engaging story that Winfield Scott narrowly escaped capture by
British skirmishers while being entertained to breakfast by "Mrs. Street".
This account was first published in the *Army and Navy Journal,* 9 June
1866, shortly after Scott's death, by a contributor who stated he obtained it
from the general in 1865.[9] Scott's biographer, Charles W. Elliott, a very
careful scholar, termed the story an "anecdote" but included it in his 1937
work, *Winfield Scott. The Soldier and the Man.*

According to Elliott, on 4 July 1814, Mrs. Street, "the wife of the
farmer through whose land the Creek flowed to the Niagara," asked Scott
for a "safeguard" for the protection of her property which the young general
freely granted. In gratitude, the lady invited Scott and his staff for breakfast
the following morning of 5 July, at her farmhouse and Scott had just seated
himself at her table

> when young George Watts, rising to get his handkerchief
> from his cap, happened to glance through the open win-
> dow. What he saw caused him to startle the breakfasters
> with a yell of alarm. "General! We are betrayed! In three
> minutes this house will be surrounded by Indians!"
> Upsetting his chair and abandoning his cocked hat on a
> side table the Brigadier dashed for the door, cleared the
> porch and steps at a bound, and, followed by Watts,
> Worth, and Smith [members of his staff], ran for his life.
> British Indians were pouring into the clearing and nearing
> the house. It was a close call, but the hatless fleers made
> the bridge and safety by a burst of creditable if undignified
> speed.[10]

There is an old saying – "It may not be the truth but it makes a good story" – that applies to this dramatic episode. In connection with it, a number of points must be made. First, Scott (never a man to suffer from the sin of modesty) did not include it in his memoirs although he included numerous other such stories, some of which are true. Second, although the evidence is sketchy, it appears that Samuel Street's wife was dead by 1814 and that the only lady on the farm was his daughter, Mary Ussher, who lived in a frame house north of the creek. It is known that Mary Ussher, on Riall's orders, drove the cattle on the farm north of the Chippawa on the afternoon of 4 July 1814 and she probably remained there in safety.[11] Third, no other American source, particularly those of Captain Joseph Henderson of the Twenty-Second Infantry or Captain Benjamin Ropes of the Twenty-First Infantry, whose companies were on picket in the vicinity of the Street/Ussher house that morning, mention the presence of Canadian civilians there. Fourth, neither officer mentions the incident and, more importantly, neither mentions British warriors approaching that close to the house. There being reasons sufficient to question the story's veracity, it has not been included in the main text.

4. The Fate of Lieutenant Colonel Robert Bull of Fenton's Regiment
Lieutenant Colonel Robert Bull of Fenton's Pennsylvania Volunteer regiment was killed after being taken prisoner by British warriors. Captain Samuel White, who witnessed Bull's death, thought that

> the murder was committed in compliance with order of General Rial [sic], who had given the Indians positive instructions not to spare any who wore the uniform of militia officers, he at the same time gave them a minute description of the dress of the militia and regular officer, the latter of whom, should any be captured, they were ordered to bring into camp in safety ...
>
> That we were not murdered as we expected, was owing to our being dressed in the uniform of regular troops, with which we had provided ourselves before our departure from Gettysburg – the unfortunate Colonel was dressed in the old uniform of the Pennsylvania militia, and met his disastrous fate in consequence of a trifling inattention – so frail and slender are the threads upon which human life and human prosperity are dependent.[12]

This author has never found, in either British official records or manuscript sources, an order such as that described by White or even mention of such an order. It is more likely that Bull's death was the result of a personal act.

According to White, Bull was killed about a half a mile from where he was captured near the skirt of the woods bordering the plain. Either his body was never found or it was not recognized by the burial parties because Bull was listed "missing" in the American casualty reports.

In October 1814, four months after the battle, Bull's fate was still a mystery and his distraught father wrote a poignant letter to Colonel Charles K. Gardner, the adjutant-general of the Left Division:[13]

> Sir
>
> Permit the father of Lieut. Col. Bull (of the Pennsylvania Volunteers) to address a line to you requesting you if possible to obtain correct information respecting the fate of that unfortunate young man who was missing at the battle of Chippawa, various statements hath come to us but none which appears to be satisfactory. The general Opinion of the Volunteers that remained with Genl. Browns Army was that he was killed. But Captain Moreland's men who guarded the prisoners to Greenbush was informed by some of said prisoners that Col. Bull, Major Galloway & Capt. White was all prisoners with the British.
>
> Having seen Col. Boerstler a few days ago who directed me to you for information as he believed you had or could Obtain that which I could depend upon, I have taken the liberty of requesting from you a statement of any facts you may be in possession of or are in any way able to obtain concerning those three Officers that were missing as above – you will please to write if any information comes to you that may be depended on directing your letter to me near Millerstown, Cumberland County, Pennsylvania.
>
> Henry Bull
> Adjt. Genl. Gardner
> 24th October 1814

5. The British Infantry Attacked in Column Formation

Many historians have written that Riall's infantry attacked in a column formation at Chippawa, not in line as described above. The evidence, however, strongly supports the British use of the line as their attack formation.

Lieutenant Colonel George Hay, the Marquis of Tweeddale, remembered that his 100th Foot formed on the plain "with its left on the river" while "the 1st Regiment formed line on my right."[14] Tweeddale was annoyed because in some preliminary manoeuvres, his companies had become reversed and "the gre[n]adiers became the left company" which meant that they formed on his left flank near the Niagara rather than in their more normal position on the right flank of the battalion.

Two other British participants confirm Tweeddale's statement. Private George Ferguson of the 100th Foot remembered being "drawn up in the open field without any defence."[15] He also recorded receiving orders to "reserve our fire until command should be given, the design being to charge them" and then "*The whole line* received the order to fire a volley."[16] Sergeant James Commins of the 8th Foot was even more specific: "The Americans must have lost a great number as they were so strongly wedged up in phalanx whereas ours was *in two complete lines*, and in that position [formation] retreated deliberately to our own ground."[17]

Finally, there are two British commentators who may not have been present but had the opportunity to talk to men who were at the battle. An early historian of the war, David Thompson, a veteran of the 1st Foot, wrote that "the main body of the British army was formed in line, which, when compared with that of the enemy, presented more the appearance of the wing of a regiment than an opposing army."[18] This is a reference to the fact that Scott's line overlapped that of the 1st and 100th Foot on the west. Lieutenant John Lang of the 19th Light Dragoons recorded that "the Royals [1st Foot] & the 100th display[ed] & advance in line with the 8th in reserve in a line" but "the line [was] opposed by high numbers and obliged to retire."[19]

American witnesses are just as positive. Baker of the Canadian Volunteers wrote that "the British columns advanced and displayed on their Right & left their line extending from the River to their flank in the woods."[20] Scott, who had reason to be particular, recorded in his memoirs that, at the commencement of the battle on the plain, the "Two hostile lines were now in view of each other" and then gave details of the tactical movements he made to take the oncoming British line in the flank.[21] Finally, Jesup of the Twenty-Fifth Infantry described how McNeil's Eleventh Infantry "attacked in flank that part of the enemy line which still maintained its ground."[22]

If the evidence is this strong why have historians concluded that Riall's infantry attacked in column? The source of their error appears to be a sentence in the British general's official report where he states that: "The troops moved in three columns, the third (the King's Regiment) being in advance."[23] But this is a reference, not to attack columns, but to the columns of march formed by the three British battalions on their way from the bridge over the Chippawa to their deployment on the plain. There is an important distinction between the two – the column of march was deeper than it was wide while the attack column, basically a thickened line, was wider than it was deep.

The first historian who seems to have fallen into this error was Charles Elliott who, in 1937, described the British formation as being "a line of columns" and whose map of the battle shows the British regiments in three distinct columns.[24] Jeffrey Kimball, who made an intensive study of the battle in an article published in 1967, did not copy this error but the map that accompanied his work might be misconstrued to represent two British attack columns moving on an American line.[25]

More recent authors, using Kimball as their source on the battle but, apparently, not reading him closely, have concluded that the British attacked in column and the Americans defended in line. In his 1981 work, *Flames Across the Border*, author Pierre Berton not only confused column and line formations but provided a map showing the British attacking in columns of march.[26] Finally, George Stanley, writing in 1983, states that Riall made use of the "column approach characteristic of French infantry tactics," but he confused attack columns with columns of march and includes a map of the battle showing the flanks of the American line wheeled so far that they are, in effect, firing into their own ranks.[27]

6. The Origin of the Expression "Why, These are Regulars!"

One of the most popular anecdotes of the battle is that the British, on first seeing the grey uniforms of Scott's brigade, mistook them for militia dressed in the grey homespun, common to farmers throughout North America. Riall, on seeing the steady, unfaltering movements of the grey-clad enemy, is said to have realized his mistake and exclaimed: "These are regulars!," or words to that effect.

This expression has become an integral part of the mythology of the battle, but there is no British or Canadian source that confirms Riall's use of these words. In fact, the only source the author has been able to find is Winfield Scott himself. Writing in 1864, the Scott stated that

General Riall, who had dispersed twice his numbers the winter before, in his expedition on the American side, said: *It is nothing but a body of Buffalo militia!* But when the bridge was passed in fine style, under his heavy fire of artillery, he added with an oath: *Why, these are regulars!*[28]

The original has been embellished somewhat – by 1937, Elliott gives it as: "Those are regulars, by God!," and he has been followed by others.[29]

Notes

Abbreviations Used in Notes

AO   Archives of Ontario, Toronto, Canada
ASPMA   *American State Papers. Class V, Military Affairs.* Washington: Gales
            & Seaton, 1832. Document cited first, followed by
            volume, and page number.
BECHS   Buffalo and Erie County Historical Society
CL   Clements Library, University of Michigan
CHS   Connecticut Historical Society
DCB   *Dictionary of Canadian Biography*
Doc. Hist.   Ernest A. Cruikshank, ed., *Documentary History of the Campaigns
            upon the Niagara Frontier in 1812-1814.* Welland: Tribune Press,
            1896-1908.
LC   Library of Congress, Washington
LDOB   Left Division Order Book, New York State Library, Albany
LL   Lilly Library, University of Indiana
MHS   Mississippi Department of Archives and History
MG   Manuscript Group
NA   National Archives of Canada
NYSL   New York State Library
PLDU   Perkins Library, Duke University
PRO   Public Record Office
RG   Record Group
USMHI   United States Military History Institute
USNA   United States National Archives
WO   War Office

Chapter 1: War Comes to the Niagara, 1812-1814

1   On Glegg's mission, see Casselman, *Richardson's War of 1812*, 11-12. On mess life at Fort George, see: Landmann, *Adventures and Recollections*, II, 52-54; Maude, *Visit to the Falls of Niagara in 1800*, 120; Niagara Historical Society Publication No. 11, "Reminiscences of Niagara," 10.

2   Prevost to Drummond, 30 April 1814 quoted in Hitsman, *Incredible War*, 184.

3   Prevost to Brock, 8 July 1812 quoted in Hitsman, *Incredible War*, 156. Strength of British forces in Upper Canada from WO 17, vols. 1516 and 2359, General Returns of the Army, NA.

4   Brock to Prevost, 25 February 1812, RG 8 I, vol. 676, 239, NA.

5   Vincent to Prevost, 19 May 1813, RG 8 I, vol. 678, 301, NA.

6   Petition to Vincent, 19 May 1813, Riddell, "Willcocks," 497-498n.

7   Norton, *Journal*, 325.

8   Armstrong to Boyd, 7 July 1813, RG 107, micro 6, reel 7, USNA.

9   Porter to Armstrong, 27 July 1813, RG 107, micro 221, reel 8, USNA.

10   Willcocks to Boyd, 19 July 1813, RG 94, entry 125, USNA.

11 Merritt, *Journal*, 45. On Willcocks in the autumn of 1813, see General Orders, Newark, 14 November 1813, RG 8 I, vol. 1201, 69-70, NA; Merritt, *Journal*, 42-45; Harrison to Armstrong, 14 November 1813, RG 107, micro 221, reel 53, USNA.

12 "Chapin to the Public," *Buffalo Gazette*, 14 June 1814.

Chapter 2: "Grey Jackets"

1 Graves, *Lundy's Lane*, 8.

2 Clark to Eustis, 4 June 1813, RG 107, micro 222, reel 5, USNA.

3 Heitman, *Register*, 50-142; Statement of the Graduates of the Military Academy, *ASPMA*, IV, 52-57; Stagg, *Madison's War*, 167; Roach, "Journal," 131.

4 Crombie, "McFarland," 105.

5 Graves, "Handsome Army," 46. Although its official designation was the 1st Division of the 9th Military District, Brown's army was usually referred as the Left Division and that term has been used in the text.

6 Letter in the *Columbian Centinel*, 16 September 1815. Additional material on Brown from Morris, "Brown."

7 Charles Elliott has written the best biography of Winfield Scott. See Elliott, *Scott*.

8 Fredriksen, *Officers*, 77-78.

9 Fredriksen, *Officers*, 97-98.

10 Cate, "Ropes," 116. On the training of the Left Division at Flint Hill, see Graves, "Handsome Army."

11 Brigade Order, 23 June 1814, LDOB, NYSL.

12 Chartrand, *Uniforms*, 42-50; General Orders, 19 May and 24 May 1814, LDOB, NYSL.

13 Scott to Winder, 6 May 1814, Elliott, *Scott*, 148.

14 Strength figures of Left Division, first week of July 1814, extracted from: "Strength of Major General Brown's Army, Buffalo, July 1, 1814," Adams, *History*, VIII, 37; Whitehorne, *Fort Erie*, Annex D.

15 McMullen, "Narrative," Cruikshank, *Doc. Hist.*, II, 368-379; Memorandum of Amasiah Ford, USMHI; Biography of Jarvis Hanks, BECHS. The author is editing the memoirs of these three enlisted men for publication.

16 Stagg, "Enlisted Men," 645; Pay from *Army Register*, 106.

17 Stagg, "Enlisted Men," 615-645; ages and sizes of soldiers from Schneider, "Training and Organization," 33-34; colour of hair and eyes from RG 8 I, vols. 694A & B, Prisoner of War Ledgers, Quebec, 1814, NA.

18 Whitehorne, *Fort Erie*, 50, 70.

19 Description of uniform of the First Brigade from Chartrand, *Uniforms*, 42-50, 103-104.

20 Scott, *Memoirs*, I, 119.

21 Jesup, "Memoir," LC.

22 Hanks, "Biography," BECHS.

Chapter 3: "Red Coats"

1 Riall, *DCB*, VII, 744-746.

2 Graves, *Lundy's Lane*, 46-49.

3 Graves, *Lundy's Lane*, 49.

4   Riall's strength from "Abstract of Weekly Distribution Return of the Right
      Division, 22 June 1814," Cruikshank, *Doc. Hist.*, I, 28.

5   Abstract of Weekly Distribution Return of the Right Division, 22 June 1814,
      Cruikshank, *Doc. Hist.*, I, 28; Mackonochie to Maclachlane, 11 July 1814, WO
      55, vol. 1223, 311, NA.

6   M. Glover, *Wellington as Commander*, 24-28. On the Duke of York's reforms,
      see R. Glover, *Peninsular Preparation*.

7   *General Regulations*, 31.

8   Service of lieutenants of 1st Foot extrapolated from the *Army List, 1814*.

9   Hendry, "Casualties at Chippawa," Annexes A & C.

10   Punishment records of the 8th Foot from Inspection Return of the 8th Foot,
      WO 27, vol. 133, PRO; Coss, "British Soldier," 245.

11   Coss, "British Soldier," 244-245; Ferguson, "Journal"; WO 27, vol. 133,
      Inspection Return of the 8th Foot, 1815, PRO.

12   List of Warriors who have gone to Fort George, 24 June 1814, RG 10, vol. 28,
      17032, NA; "Norton," *DCB*, VI, 550-553.

13   Couture, "Non-Regular Forces," 141-142.

14   MacEwen, *Excerpts*, 6.

15   Lord, "Commins," 211.

Chapter 4: The Trade and Its Tools

1   Blackmore, *Fire-Arms*, 277; Gluckman, *U.S. Muskets*, 64-66; Hicks, *Notes*, I,
      19.

2   Hughes, *Firepower*, 133; Greener, *The Gun*, 222.

3   Hughes, *Firepower*, 127-133.

4   My description of infantry tactics during the War of 1812 is taken from:
      Graves, *Lundy's Lane*, 23-28; *Rules and Regulations*, 63-78; Smyth, *Regulations*,
      1-3, 29, 59; Colin, *La Tactique*, xvii-cii; Griffith, *Forward*, 25-31; and Strachan,
      Waterloo to Balaclava, 26-29.

5   Jackson, *View of the Armies*, 176. On the function of light infantry during this
      period, see Fuller, *Moore's System*.

6   Horton, "Original Narrative," 19.

7   Unless otherwise noted, my description of the weapons and tactics of artillery
      during the War of 1812 is extracted from Graves, "Artillery."

8   Hughes, *Open Fire*, 13; Hughes, *Firepower*, 38, 164; Adye, *Bombardier*, 195,
      300; Tousard, *Companion*, II, 252.

9   Du Teil, *Artillerie Nouvelle*, 26. Original in French, the translation is mine.

10   Hughes, *Firepower*, 126.

11   I am indebted to Major Jean Morin of the Royal 22e Régiment for this infor-
      mation.

12   Anonymous, *Journal of a Soldier of the Seventy First Regiment* (London, 1822)
      quoted in Richardson, *Fighting Spirit*, 7.

13   Moran, *Anatomy*, 69.

14   Anonymous, "First Campaign," 75.

15   Campbell, "Ideas about Battle."

Chapter 5: "An excitement among the people"

1   Cate, "Ropes," 116-117; Porter to Stone, 26 May 1840, Cruikshank, *Doc. Hist.*,
      II, 361; Brown, "Memoranda," NYSL; Jesup, "Memoir," LC.

2 Scott, *Memoir*, I, 123; Instructions of Commanding Officer, Fort Erie, 12 May 1814, Riall Letter book, BECHS.

3 Scott, *Memoir*, I, 123.

4 Brown, "Memoranda," NYSL; Porter to Stone, 27 May 1840, Cruikshank, *Doc. Hist.* I, 361; Hanks, "Biography," BECHS.

5 Brown, "Memoranda," NYSL.

6 Henderson, "Narrative," LL.

7 Jesup, "Memoir," LC; White, *History*, 12.

8 Instructions to Commanding Officer, Fort Erie, 12 May 1814, Riall Letter book, BECHS.

9 Merritt, *Journal*, 77.

10 Cate, "Ropes," 116-117.

11 Return of the British prisoners of war, 3 July 1814, Cruikshank, *Doc. Hist.*, I, 42.

12 Riall to Drummond, 6 July 1814, RG 8 I, vol. 684, 51, NA.

13 Merritt, *Journal*, 55.

14 Ferguson, "Journal," 58.

15 Norton, *Journal*, 348-349.

16 Clinton, *Journal*, quoted in Seibel, *Portage Road*, 215.

17 Mrs. Simcoe's Diary quoted in Seibel, *Portage Road*, 207.

18 Carmichael-Smyth, *Precis*, 178; Extract of Captain Martin's Report on the Defences in Upper Canada, 3 July 1814, RG 8 I, vol. 388, 139, NA.

19 Riall to Drummond, 6 July 1814, RG 8 I, vol. 684, 51, NA; Thompson, *History*, 223.

20 Cate, "Ropes," 117; Brown to Armstrong, 7 July 1814, Cruikshank, *Doc. Hist.*, I, 38.

21 Cate, "Ropes," 117; number of horses in Left Division from Whitehorne, *Fort Erie*, Annex Q.

22 On Pearson, see Irving, *British Officers*, 29; Dunlop, *Tiger Dunlop*, 27. On Pearson's delaying action, see Scott, *Memoir*, I, 124; Riall to Drummond, 6 July 1814, RG 8 I, vol. 684, 51, NA; Jesup, "Memoir," LC.

23 Scott to adjutant general, 15 July 1814, Cruikshank, *Doc. Hist.*, I, 44.

24 Account of Crooker's action from: Jesup, "Memoir," LC; Scott to adjutant general, 15 July 1814, Cruikshank, *Doc. Hist.*, I, 44; Biddulph, *Nineteenth*, 197-198; Thompson, *History*, 223; Riall to Drummond, 6 July 1814, RG 8 I, vol. 684, 51, NA.

25 Norton, *Journal*, 349.

26 Scott, *Memoir*, I, 123; Thompson, *History*, 223.

27 Cate, "Ropes," 117; Brown to Armstrong, 7 July 1814, Cruikshank, *Doc. Hist.*, I, 38.

Chapter 6: "We had considerable Scirmushing the foornoon"

1 Brown to Armstrong, 7 July 1814, Cruikshank, *Doc. Hist.*, I, 38.

2 Wilkinson, *Memoirs*, I, 650.

3 "Sketch of Biddle," 554; Hanks, "Biography," BECHS; Map No. 11, Wilkinson, *Diagrams*; Plan of Battle of Chippewa, USNA, RG 77, Drawing 154, Sheet 42-24.

4 "Sketch of Biddle," 554.

5 Account of Street and the Grove Farm from: *DCB*, V, 781-782; Statement of Property Belonging to the Late Samuel Street, 21 October 1815, RG 19 E5(a), vol. 3751, claim 506, NA; Graves, "Human Remains," II, 22-37.

6 Scott, *Memoirs*, I, 127.

7 Hanks, "Biography," BECHS.

8 Einstein, "Tweeddale," 73.

9 Einstein, "Tweeddale," 73.

10 Wilkinson, *Memoirs*, I, 650 and 650n.

11 Porter to Stone, 26 May 1840, Cruikshank, *Doc. Hist.* II, 362.

12 Henderson, "Narrative," LL.

13 Cate, "Ropes," 117-118.

14 Treat, *Vindication*, 33-34; "Sketch of Biddle," 554; Wilkinson, *Memoirs*, I, 659.

15 General Order, Chippewa, 5 July 1814, LDOB, NYSL.

16 Jesup, "Memoir," LC: Brown to Armstrong, 7 July 1814, Cruikshank, *Doc. Hist.*, I, 38.

17 Norton, *Journal*, 349.

18 Drummond to Prevost, 12 July 1814, Cruikshank, *Doc. Hist.*, I, 35.

19 Merritt, *Journal*, 56.

20 Riall's strength from Merritt, *Journal*, 56; Mackonochie to Maclachlane, 11 July 1814, WO 55, vol. 1223, 311, NA; marginal notations on Riall to Drummond, 6 July 1814, RG 8 I, vol. 684, 51, NA; Drummond to Prevost, 12 July 1814, Cruikshank, *Doc. Hist.*, I, 35.

21 Norton, *Journal*, 349-350.

22 Couture, "Non-Military Forces," 141-142.

23 Green, "Township No. 2," 286-287, 297; Green, *Some Graves*, 48-50; Biggar, *Tale*, n.p; Graves, *Lundy's Lane*, 103-104; Return of the Militia Men Killed and Wounded, 5 July 1814, RG 9, 1B4, vol 1, 98-99, NA.

24 Ferguson, "Journal," 58-59.

25 Einstein, "Tweeddale," 71-72.

26 McMullen, "Narrative," in Cruikshank, *Doc. Hist.*, II, 372-373; Porter to Stone, 26 May 1840, Cruikshank, *Doc. Hist.* II, 362-363.

27 Porter to Stone, 26 May 1840, Cruikshank, *Doc. Hist.*, II, 362.

28 Porter to Stone, 26 May 1840, Cruikshank, *Doc. Hist.*, II, 362.

Chapter 7: "Scenes of indescribable horror"

1 White, *History*, 14.

2 White, *History*, 14.

3 Porter to Stone, 26 May 1840, Cruikshank, *Doc. Hist.*, II, 363.

4 McMullen, "Narrative," in Cruikshank, *Doc. Hist.*, II, 373.

5 White, *History*, 14.

6 Porter to Stone, 26 May 1840, Cruikshank, *Doc. Hist.*, II, 363. Also Wilkinson, *Memoirs*, I, 651; White, *History*, 15; Porter to Brown, n.d. [c. 12-15 July 1814], Cruikshank, *Doc. Hist.*, II, 410; Letter from a captain in Fenton's regiment, *Columbian Centinel*, 28 July 1814.

7 Porter to Stone, 26 May 1840, Cruikshank, *Doc. Hist.*, II, 363.

8 Porter to Stone, 26 May 1840, Cruikshank, *Doc. Hist.*, II, 363-364.

9 Brown, "Memoranda," NYSL.

10 Cate, "Ropes," 118; Gardner to Brown, 10 March 1825, Gardner Papers, NYSL.

11 Porter to Stone, 26 May 1840, Cruikshank, *Doc. Hist.*, II, 364.

12 Ferguson, "Journal," 60. Also Merritt, *Journal*, 56; Norton, *Journal*, 349; Thompson, *History*, 225; Lang, "Diary," PLDU; Riall to Drummond, 6 July 1814, RG 8 I, vol. 684, 51, NA.

13 Merritt, *Journal*, 56; Norton, *Journal*, 49; Letter from a captain in Fenton's regiment, *Columbian Centinel*, 13 August 1814.

14 Porter to Stone, 26 May 1840, Cruikshank, *Doc. Hist.*, II, 364; Merritt, *Journal*, 56.

15 Dickson to Coffin, 7 March 1820, RG 9, IB1, vol. 8, NA.

16 Dickson, *DCB*, VII, 222; Return of the Militia Men Killed and Wounded, 6 July 1814, RG 9, IB4, vol. 1, 98, NA; Merritt, *Journal*, 56.

17 Porter to Stone, 26 May 1840, Cruikshank, *Doc. Hist.*, II, 364; Norton, *Journal*, 350.

18 Norton, *Journal*, 350.

19 Letter printed in *Federal Gazette and Baltimore Daily Advertizer*, 2 August 1814.

20 White, *History*, 18. By "light horse," White meant the British light dragoons, which were moving onto the plain.

21 White, *History*, 17.

22 McMullen, "Narrative," in Cruikshank, *Doc. Hist.*, II, 373.

23 Porter to Stone, 26 May 1840, Cruikshank, *Doc. Hist.*, II, 365.

24 Armstrong to Brown, 7 July 1814, Cruikshank, *Doc. Hist.*, I, 39.

25 Gardner to Brown, 10 March 1825, Gardner Papers, NYSL.

Chapter 8: "Why, these are Regulars!"

1   Scott, *Memoirs*, I, 127-128.

2   Gardner to Brown, 10 March 1825, Gardner Papers, NYSL.

3   Scott, *Memoirs*, I, 128.

4   Gardner to Brown, 10 March 1825, Gardner Papers, NYSL.

5   Riall to Drummond, 6 July 1814, RG 8 I, vol. 684, 51, NA; Einstein, "Tweeddale," 78; Norton, *Journal*, 349; Mackonochie to Maclachlane, 11 July 1814, WO 55, vol. 1223, 311, NA; Lang, "Diary," 29 June 1814, PLDU.

6   Ferguson, "Journal," 59-60; British troop strengths from Riall to Drummond, 6 July 1814, marginal notations by Drummond, RG 8 I, vol. 684, 51, NA; Drummond to Prevost, 12 July 1814, Cruikshank, *Doc. Hist.*, I, 35.

7   Einstein, "Tweeddale," 72-74.

8   Askwith, *Kane's List*, 39; *Army List 1814*; Mackonochie to Maclachlane, 11 July 1814, WO 55, vol. 1223, 311, NA; Dunlop, *Tiger Dunlop*, 40-41; Return of the Brass Guns, Quebec, 30 April 1807, WO 44, vol. 250, 14, NA.

9   Cate, "Ropes," 117.

10 Livingston, *Sketches*, 400.

11 Hanks, "Memoir," BECHS.

12 Cate, "Ropes," 117.

13 Scott to Adjutant General, 12 July 1814, Cruikshank, *Doc. Hist.*, I, 44. Also, Henderson, "Narrative," LL.

14 Fredriksen, *Officers*, 60-61, 150, fn26.

15 Graves, *Lundy's Lane*, 32-33.

16 Fredriksen, *Gallery*, 73-74.

17 Jesup, "Memoir," LC. Also Jesup to Brown, 12 July 1814, Gardner Papers, NYSL.

18 Scott, *Memoirs*, I, 130; Kimball, "Chippewa," 181; Weekes to Livermore, 9 February 1825, Douglass Papers, CL.

19   Livingston, *Sketches*, 400; Fredriksen, *Officers*, 125-126.

20   Mackonochie to Maclachlane, 11 July 1814, WO 55, vol. 1223, 311, NA.

21   Mackonochie to Maclachlane, 11 July 1814, WO 55, vol. 1223, 311, NA.

22   Kimball, "Chippewa," 481.

23   Scott, *Memoirs*, I, 128. This appears to be the only source for this famous exclamation.

24   Ferguson, "Journal," 59.

25   Riall to Drummond, 6 July 1814, RG 8 I, vol. 684, 51, NA.

26   *Rules and Regulations*, 220-221.

27   Swinson, *Register*, 73-74; Chichester and Burges-Short, *Records*, 189-190.

28   Chichester and Burges-Short, *Records*, 246-247; Evans, *DCB*, IX, 246.

29   Chichester and Burges-Short, *Records*, 826-827.

30   Lord, "Commins," 208.

31   Information on Fenton and Fearon from Hendry, "Casualties," Annex A.

32   Ferguson, "Memoir," 60. O'Flanagan was court-martialled for his actions at Chippawa and cashiered, see General Court Martial, Montreal, 18 February 1815, RG 8 I, vol. 167, 197, NA. Brereton was also court-martialled for his actions at Chippawa, but the court accepted his plea that he fell behind his regiment because of exhaustion. See Torrens to Prevost, 17 June 1815, RG 8 I, vol. 167, 79, NA.

33   General Order, Right Division, 1 August 1814, RG 8 I, vol. 231, 128, NA. Although dated after the battle, this order confirmed orders issued previous to the action.

34   Fredriksen, *Officers*, 65-66.

35   Scott, *Memoirs*, I, 129.

36   Scott, *Memoirs*, I, 131; Livingston, *Sketches*, 400.

37   Scott, *Memoirs*, I, 134n.

38   Scott, *Memoirs*, I, 131. Scott estimated that the distance between the two lines was 60-70 paces (a pace is 2 1/2 feet) or 150 and 175 feet. Randolph, "Autobiography," MHS, states that the two lines were between 60 and 70 yards, or 180 and 210 feet.

Chapter 9: "The slaughter was great"

1   Ferguson, "Memoir," 60.

2   Cate, "Ropes," 118.

3   Scott to adjutant general, 12 July 1814, Cruikshank, *Doc. Hist.*, I, 44.

4   Stone, *Red Jacket*, 264.

5   Randolph, "Autobiography," MHS.

6   Stevenson to Addison, July 1814, Niagara Historical Society Papers, AO.

7   Hanks, "Biography," BECHS.

8   Ferguson, "Memoir," 60.

9   Mackonochie to Glasgow, 19 August 1814, WO 55, vol. 1224, 332, NA. Towson's casualties from Report of the killed and wounded of the left division, 5 July 1814, Cruikshank, *Doc. Hist.*, I, 43.

10   Gardner to Brown 10 March 1825, Gardner Papers, NYSL.

11   Wilkinson, *Memoirs*, I, 651; Treat, *Vindication*, 15-16.

12   Porter to Stone, 27 May 1840, Cruikshank, *Doc. Hist.*, II, 365.

13   "Sketch of Hindman," 44.

14   Hindman to adjutant general, n.d., Cruikshank, *Doc. Hist.*, I, 44.

15   Brown, "Memoranda," NYSL.

16   Jesup to Brown, 12 July 1814, draft in Gardner Papers, NYSL; Jesup, "Memoir," LC; George Howard Letter book, 110-111, CHS.

17   Jesup to Brown, 12 July 1814, draft in Gardner Papers, NYSL.

18   Howard, "Letter book," 110, CHS.

19   Jesup to Brown, draft in Gardner Papers, NYSL.

20   Jesup to Brown, 12 July 1814, draft in Gardner Papers, NYSL.

21   *Biography of John McNeil,* quoted in Fredriksen, *Officers,* 65.

22   Henderson, "Narrative," LL.

23   Stevenson to Addison, July 1812, Niagara Historical Society Papers, AO.

24   Ridout to Ridout, 10 July 1814, Edgar, *Ten Years,* 288; Stevenson to Addison, July 1812, Niagara Historical Society Papers, AO.

25   Hendry, "Casualties," Annex A.

26   Henderson, "Narrative," LL.

27   Einstein, "Tweeddale," 73.

28   Ridout to Ridout, 10 July 1814, Edgar, *Ten Years,* 288.

29   Ridout to Ridout, 10 July 1812, Edgar, *Ten Years,* 288; *Army List 1814;* Einstein, "Tweeddale," 73.

30   Ferguson, "Journal," 60.

31   Ferguson, "Journal," 61.

32   Scott to adjutant general, 15 July 1814, Cruikshank, *Doc. Hist.,* I, 46. Also, Brown, "Memoranda," NYSL.

33   Scott, *Memoirs,* I, 131; Drummond to Prevost, 10 July 1814, Cruikshank, *Doc. Hist.,* I, 35.

34   Lord, "Commins," 208; Riall to Drummond, 6 July 1814, RG 8 I, vol. 684, 51, NA.

35   Howard, Letter book, CHS. Also, Einstein, "Tweeddale," 73.

36   White, *History,* 24.

37   Norton, *Journal,* 350.

38   Baker, "Memory Book," 5 July 1814, MG 24, G17, NA.

39   McMullen, "Narrative," in Cruikshank, *Doc. Hist.,* II, 373.

40   Porter to Stone, 26 May 1840, Cruikshank, *Doc. Hist.,* II, 373; Stone, *Red Jacket,* 264.

41   Gardner to Brown, 10 March 1825, Gardner Papers, NYSL.

42   Brown to Armstrong, 7 July 1814, Cruikshank, *Doc. Hist.,* I, 38.

Chapter 10: "It was painful to witness the distress and agony"

1   Return of the Killed, Wounded and Missing of the Right Division, appended to Riall to Drummond, 6 July 1814, RG 8 I, vol. 684, 51, NA.

2   Return of the killed, wounded and prisoners of the enemy, Inspector-General's Office, 9 July 1814, Cruikshank, *Doc. Hist.,* I, 42.

3   Report of the killed and wounded of the Left Division, 5 July 1814, Cruikshank, *Doc. Hist.,* I, 43.

4   Graves, "Human Remains," I; Hendry, "Casualties."

5   Cate, "Ropes," 119.

6   Cate, "Ropes," 119.

7   Whitehorne, *Fort Erie,* Annex P; Cate, "Ropes," 119; Henderson, "Narrative," LL.

8   Merritt, *Journal,* 56.

9   Ferguson, "Journal," 62.

10   Graves, "Human Remains," II, 91-94; Letter from a captain in Fenton's Regiment to his brother in Carlisle, 7 July 1814, *Columbian Centinel,* 28 July 1814; Cate, "Ropes," 119; General Order, 6 July 1814, LDOB, NYSL.

11   Merritt, *Journal,* 57.

12   White, *History,* 25.

13   On native concepts of warfare, see Benn, "Iroquois Warfare."

14   On Porter and his native subordinates' treatment of the enemy dead and wounded, see Porter to Stone, 26 May 1840, Cruikshank, *Doc. Hist.,* II, 366-367.

15   Riall to Drummond, 6 July 1814, RG 8 I, vol. 684, 51, NA.

16   Drummond to Prevost, 10 July 1814, Cruikshank, *Doc. Hist.,* I, 35.

17   Prevost to Drummond, 12 July 1814, RG 8 I, vol. 1222, 162, NA.

18   Prevost to Glasgow, 26 August 1814, WO 55, vol. 1222, 338, NA.

19   Brown to Armstrong, 7 July 1814, Cruikshank, *Doc. Hist.,* I, 38.

20   Howard, "Letter book," 112, CHS.

21   Norton, *Journal,* 351.

22   Lord, "Commins," 208.

23   Merritt, *Journal,* 56.

24   Merritt, *Journal,* 56-57.

Chapter 11: The Long and Bloody Summer of 1814

1   Unless otherwise noted, my account of the remainder of the Niagara campaign of 1814 is based on Graves, *Lundy's Lane,* and Whitehorne, *Fort Erie.*

Epilogue

1   Unless otherwise noted, the postwar history of the battlefield is from Graves, "Human Remains," II, 22-40.

2   Mermet to Viger, 31 July 1814, Viger Papers, Vol. 4, 58, Microfilm M-8, NA. The original is in French, the translation is mine.

3   Graves, "Human Remains," I.

Appendix F

1   Scott, *Memoirs,* I, 129.

2   Lossing, *Field Book,* 806n.

3   Chartrand, *Uniforms,* 53.

4   Thompson, *History,* 227.

5   Kirby, *Annals,* 204.

6   Kirby, *Annals,* 207.

7   For evidence of the American burial of the British dead, see: Brown, "Memoranda," NYSL; Jesup, "Memoir," LC; White, *History,* 24-25; Baker, "Memory Book," 6 July 1814, NA; Witherow, "Diary," 6 July 1814.

8   For a description of the disposition of the dead after the battle of Lundy's Lane, see Graves, *Lundy's Lane,* Chapter 11.

9   Elliott, *Scott,* 158.

10 Elliott, *Scott,* 158.

11 Statement of Property belonging to the Estate of the late Samuel Street ... Plundered and Destroyed by the Enemy, 21 October 1815, RG 19 E5(A), vol. 3751, file 3, claim 506, NA.

12 White, *History,* 19.

13   Bull to Gardner, 24 October 1814, Gardner Papers, NYSL.

14   Einstein, "Tweeddale," 73.

15   Ferguson, "Journal," 59.

16   Ferguson, "Journal," 60. The emphasis is mine.

17   Lord, "Commins," 208. The emphasis is mine.

18   Thompson, *History*, 225.

19   Lang, "Diary," 29 June 1814, PLDU.

20   Baker, "Memory Book," 5 July 1814, NA.

21   Scott, *Memoirs*, I, 129.

22   Jesup, "Memoir," LC.

23   Riall to Drummond, 6 July 1814, RG 8 I, vol. 684, 51, NA.

24   Elliott, *Scott*, 159, 161.

25   Kimball, "Chippewa," 168-186.

26   Berton, *Flames*, 322-323.

27   Stanley, *War of 1812*, 312-314.

28   Scott, *Memoirs*, I, 128-129.

29   Elliott, *Scott*, 162. Among other historians, see Mahon, *War of 1812*, 269: "Those are regulars, by God"; Stanley, *War of 1812*, 312: "Those are regulars, by God!"; and Elting, *Amateurs to Arms*, 186: "Those are regulars, by God!"

Bibliography
Primary Sources: Archival

Archives of Ontario, Toronto, Canada
Niagara Historical Society Papers

Buffalo and Erie County Historical Society, Buffalo, New York
Biography of Drummer Jarvis Hanks, Eleventh Infantry
Manuscripts Collection, War of 1812, Letter book of Maj. Gen. Phineas Riall

Connecticut Historical Society, Hartford, Connecticut
Letter book of Capt. George Howard, Twenty-Fifth Infantry

Library of Congress, Washington, D.C.
Thomas S. Jesup Papers, Twenty-Fifth Infantry, "Memoir of the Campaign on the Niagara"

Lilly Library, Indiana University, Bloomington, Indiana
War of 1812 Manuscripts
Narrative of Capt. Joseph Henderson, Twenty-Second Infantry

Mississippi Department of Archives & History, Jackson, Mississippi
Autobiography of Lt. Edward B. Randolph, Left Division staff

National Archives of Canada, Ottawa, Canada
Manuscript Group 24
G17, Memory Book of Joseph Baker, Canadian Volunteers
L8, Viger Papers, Ma Saberdache Bleu, vol. 4
Public Record Office Material
War Office 17, Monthly Returns
War Office 27, Inspection Returns
War Office 44, Ordnance Office, In-Letters
War Office 55, Ordnance Office, Miscellanea
Record Group 8 I, British Military and Naval Records, 1757-1903
Record Group 9, Pre-Confederation Militia Records
Record Group 10, Records of the Indian Department
Record Group 19, E5, War of 1812 Loss Board Claims

New York State Library, Albany, New York
Mss. 11225, Left Division Order Book, April-July 1814
Papers of Col. Charles K. Gardner, Left Division staff
"[Jacob Brown] Memoranda of Occurrences and Some Important Facts Attending the Campaign on the Niagara"

Perkins Library, Duke University, Durham, North Carolina
Diary of Lt. John Lang, 19th Light Dragoons

United States Army Military History Institute, Carlisle, Pennsylvania
Memorandum of Amasiah Ford, Twenty-Third Infantry

United States National Archives, Washington, D.C.
Record Group 107, Correspondence of the Secretary of War
Micro 6, Letters Sent
Micro 221, Letters Received, Registered Series
Micro 222, Letters Received, Unregistered Series
National Map Collection
Record Group 77, Drawing 154, Sheet 42-24, Plan of Battle of
Chippewa, by "Engineer of General Brown"

United Church Archives, Toronto
Journal of the Reverend George Ferguson

William L. Clements Library, University of Michigan, Ann Arbour,
Michigan
War of 1812 Papers
David B. Douglass Papers

Primary Sources: Published

Newspapers and Periodicals
American Watchman, Wilmington, Delaware
Buffalo Gazette
Columbian Centinel, Boston
Federal Gazette and Baltimore Daily Advertizer, Baltimore

Published Documents
Cruikshank, Ernest A. ed. *Documentary History of the Campaigns upon the Niagara
Frontier in 1812-1814* [titles vary slightly]. Welland: Tribune Press, 1896-
1908. 9 vols.
United States, Congress. *American State Papers. Class V, Military Affairs.* Vol. I.
Washington: Gales & Seaton, 1832.

Published Memoirs, Diaries, Journals, Correspondence

AMERICAN
Cate, Mary R., ed. "Benjamin Ropes' Autobiography," *Essex Institute Historical
Collections,* 91 (1955), 105-127.

Crombie, John N., ed. "The Papers of Daniel McFarland. A Hawk of 1812," *Western Pennsylvania Historical Magazine* 51 (1968), No. 2, 101-125.

"First Campaign of an A.D.C." *Military and Naval Magazine of the United States* 1 (1833), 153-162.

Harris, Samuel D. "Service of Capt. Samuel D. Harris; A Sketch of His Military Career as a Captain in the Second Regiment of Light Dragoons during the War of 1812," *Publications of the Buffalo Historical Society* 24 (1920), 327-342.

Horton, John F., ed. "An Original Narrative of the Niagara Campaign of 1814," *Niagara Frontier*, 46 (1964), 1-36.

McMullen, Alexander. "The Narrative of Alexander McMullen, a Private Soldier in Colonel Fenton's Regiment of Pennsylvania Volunteers." In *Documentary History of the Campaign on the Niagara in 1814*, Vol. II, 368-379. E.A. Cruikshank, ed. Welland: Tribune Press, 1896-1908 (9 vols.).

Roach, Isaac. "Journal of Major Isaac Roach, 1812-1824," *Pennsylvania Magazine of History and Biography*, XVII (1893), 129-162.

Scott, Winfield. *Memoirs of General Scott, Written by Himself.* New York: Sheldon, 1864. 2 vols.

Treat, Joseph [Twenty-First Infantry]. *The Vindication of Joseph Treat, late of the Twenty First Regiment.* Philadelphia: author, 1815.

White, Samuel [Pennsylvania Volunteers]. *A History of the American Troops during the Late War under Colonel Fenton.* Baltimore: author, 1829.

Wilkinson, James. *Memoirs of My Own Times.* Philadelphia: Abraham Small, 1816. 2 vols.

———. *Diagrams and Plans, Illustrative of the Principal Battles and Military Affairs Treated of in Memoirs of My Own Times.* Philadelphia: Abraham Small, 1816.

Witherow, John. "A Soldier's Diary for 1814," *Pennsylvania History* 12 (1945), 292-303.

BRITISH AND CANADIAN

Dunlop, William. *Tiger Dunlop's Upper Canada.* Carleton University, Toronto, 1967.

Einstein, Lewis, ed. "Recollections of the War of 1812 by George Hay, Eighth Marquis of Tweeddale." *American Historical Review* 32 (1926), 69-78.

Landmann, George Thomas. *Adventures and Recollections of Colonel Landmann, Late of the Corps of Royal Engineers.* Colburn, London, 1852. 2 vols.

Lord, Norman, ed. "The War of 1812 on the Canadian Frontier, 1812-1814. Letters written by Sergt. James Comins, 8th Foot." *Journal of the Society for Army Historical Research* 18 no. 2 (1939), 199-211.

MacEwan, William. *Excerpts from Lieut. and Adjutant William MacEwan To His Wife, Canada 1813-1814.* Arthur Brymner, ed. n.p., n.d.

Maude, John. *Visit to the Falls of Niagara in 1800.* London: Longman, Rees, Orme, Browne & Green, 1826.

Merritt, William Hamilton. *Journal of Events Principally on the Detroit and Niagara Frontiers during the War of 1812.* St. Catharines: Historical Society of British North America, 1863.

Norton, John. *The Journal of John Norton 1816.* J.J. Talman & C.F. Klinck, eds. Toronto: The Champlain Society, 1970.

Weld, Isaac. *Travels through the States of North America and the Province of Upper Canada during the Years 1795, 1796, and 1797.* London: Stockdale, 1799.

Period Military Regulations, Treatises, and Technical Literature

Adye, Ralph W. *The Bombardier and Pocket Gunner.* London: T. Egerton, 1813.

The Army Register of the United States, Corrected Up to the 1st of June, 1814. Boston: Chester Stebbins, 1814.

Du Teil, Chevalier Jean. *De L'Usage de L'Artillerie Nouvelle dans la Guerre de Campagne.* Paris: 1778 (reprinted Charles Lavauzelle, 1924).

General Regulations and Orders for the Army. London: T. Egerton, 1811.

Great Britain, War Office. *A List of all the Officers of the Army and Royal Marines on Full and half-pay.* London: War Office, 1814.

———. *Rules and Regulations for the Formation, Field-Exercise, and Movements of His Majesty's Forces.* London: T. Egerton, 1808.

Smyth, Alexander. *Rules and Regulations for the Field Exercise, Manoeuvres and Conduct of the Infantry of the United States.* Philadelphia: T. & G. Palmer, 1812.

[Stoddard, Amos]. *Exercise for Garrison and Field Ordnance, Together with Manoeuvres of Horse Artillery, as altered from the Manual of General Kosciusko, and Adapted for the Service of the United States.* Philadelphia: A. Finlay, 1812.

Tousard, Louis de. *American Artillerist's Companion, or Elements of Artillery.* Philadelphia: C. & A. Conrad, 1809. 2 vols.

Secondary Sources

Books

Adams, Henry. *History of the United States during the Administration of James Madison.* New York: A.C. Boni, 1930. 4 vols.

Askwith, W.H. *List of Officers of the Royal Regiment of Artillery From the Year 1716 to the Year 1899.* London: Royal Artillery Institution, 1900.

Berton, Pierre. *Flames across the Border, 1813-1814.* Toronto: McClelland & Stewart, 1981.

Biddulph, John. *The Nineteenth and their Times; being an Account of the Four Cavalry Regiments in the British Army that have borne the number Nineteen and of the Campaigns in which they Served.* London: John Murray, 1899.

Biggar, C.L. *A Tale of Early Days on Lundy's Lane.* Niagara Falls, Canada: n.p., n.d.

Blackmore, Howard. *British Military Firearms, 1650-1850.* London: Herbert Jenkins, 1961.

Carmichael-Smyth, James. *Precis of the Wars in Canada.* London: Tinsley Brothers, 1862.

Casselman, R.C. *Richardson's War of 1812. With Notes and a Life of the Author.* Toronto: Historical Publishing Co., 1902.

Chartrand, René. *Uniforms and Equipment of the United States Forces in the War of 1812.* Youngstown: Old Fort Niagara Association, 1992.

Chichester, Henry and George Burgess-Short. *Records and Badges of the British Army.* London: Gale & Polden, 1902.

Colin, Jean. *L'Infanterie au XVIIIe siecle: La Tactique.* Paris: Berger-Levrault, 1907.

Dictionary of Canadian Biography. Volumes V - IX. Toronto: University of Toronto, 1976-1988.

Edgar, Matilda. *Ten Years of Upper Canada in Peace and War, 1805-1815; Being the Ridout Letters with Annotations.* Toronto: William Briggs, 1890.

Elliott, Charles W. *Winfield Scott: The Soldier and the Man.* New York: MacMillan, 1937.

Elting, John. *Amateurs to Arms! A Military History of the War of 1812.* Chapel Hill: Algonquin, 1991.

Fredriksen, John C. *Officers of the War of 1812 with Portraits and Anecdotes.* Lewiston: Edgar Mellen, 1989.

Fuller, J.F.C. *Sir John Moore's System of Training.* London: 1924.

Glover, Michael. *Wellington as Military Commander.* London: Sphere, 1973.

Glover, Richard. *Peninsular Preparation: The Reform of the British Army, 1795-1809.* Cambridge: Cambridge University, 1963.

Gluckman, Arcadi. *United States Muskets, Rifles and Carbines.* Buffalo, NY: 1948.

Graves, Donald E. *The Battle of Lundy's Lane: On the Niagara, 1814.* Baltimore: Nautical & Aviation Publishing, 1993.

Green, Ernest. *Some Graves in Lundy's Lane.* Ottawa: Niagara Historical Society Publications No. 22, 1911.

Greener, William. *The Gun; or, A Treatise on the Various Descriptions of Small Fire-Arms.* London: Longman, Rees, Orme, Brown, Green, and Longman, 1835.

Griffith, Paddy. *Forward into Battle: Fighting Techniques from Waterloo to Vietnam.* Strettington: Antony Bird, 1981.

Heitman, Francis B. *Historical Register and Dictionary of the U.S Army.* Washington: Government Printing Office, 1903. 2 vols.

Hicks, James. *Notes on U.S. Ordnance.* Green Farms, Conn.: Modern Books & Craft, 1971 (reprint of 1940 edition). 2 vols.

Hitsman, J.M. *The Incredible War of 1812.* Toronto: University of Toronto, 1965.

Hughes, B.P. *Firepower: Weapons Effectiveness on the Battlefield, 1630-1850.* London: Arms and Armour, 1974.

———. *Open Fire: Artillery Tactics from Marlborough to Wellington.* Strettington: Antony Bird, 1983.

Irving, L. Homfray. *Officers of the British Forces in Canada during the War of 1812-1815.* Welland: Canadian Military Institute, 1908.

Jackson, Robert. *A Systematic View of the Formation, Discipline, and Economy of Armies.* London: 1804

Kirby, William. *Annals of Niagara.* Niagara Falls: 1896 (reprinted, Lundy's Lane Historical Society, 1972).

Laws, M.E.S. *Battery Records of the Royal Artillery, 1716-1859.* Woolwich: Royal Artillery Institute, 1952.

Livingston, John. *Sketches of Eminent Americans.* New York: Craighead, 1854.

Lossing, Benson J. *Pictorial Field Book of the War of 1812.* New York: Harpers, 1869.

Lynn, John. *Bayonets of the Republic: Motivation and Tactics in the Army of Revolutionary France, 1791-1794.* Chicago: University of Illinois, 1984.

Mahon, John K. *The War of 1812.* Gainesville: University of Florida, 1972.

Moran, Lord. *The Anatomy of Courage.* London: Constable, 1945.

Richardson, F.M. *Fighting Spirit: A Study of Psychological Factors in War.* London: Leo Cooper, 1978.

Seibel, George. *The Portage Road: 200 Years 1790-1990.* Niagara Falls: City of Niagara Falls, 1990.

Stagg, John. *Mr. Madison's War: Politics, Diplomacy, and Warfare in the Early American Republic 1783-1830.* Princeton: University Press, 1983.

Stanley, George. *The War of 1812: Land Operations.* Ottawa: National Museums, 1983.

Stewart, Charles. *The Service of British Regiments in North America.* Ottawa: Department of National Defence Library, 1962.

Stone, William L. *The Life and Times of Red Jacket.* New York: Wiley, Putnam, 1841.

Strachan, Hew. *From Waterloo to Balaclava: Tactics, Technology and the British Army, 1815-1834.* Cambridge: University Press, 1985.

Swinson, Arthur. *A Register of the Regiments and Corps of the British Army.* London: Arms & Armour, 1972.

Thompson, David. *History of the Late War Between Great Britain and the United States of America.* Niagara: T. Sewell, 1832.

Whitehorne, Joseph. *While Washington Burned: The Battle for Fort Erie, 1814.* Baltimore: Nautical & Aviation Press, 1992.

Articles

Benn, Carl. "Iroquois Warfare, 1812-1814." In *War Along the Niagara: Essays on the War of 1812 and Its Legacy.* R.A. Bowler, ed. Lewiston: Old Fort Niagara Association, 1991.

"Biographical Sketch of Major Thomas Biddle." *Illinois Monthly Magazine* 1 (1831), 549-561.

"Biographical Sketch of Colonel Jacob Hindman of the United States' Army." *Portico,* 3 (1816), 38-52.

Coss, Edward J. "The British Soldier in the Peninsular War: The Acquistion of an Unjust Reputation." *Proceedings of the Annual Meeting of the Western Society for French History* XVIII (1991), 243-251.

Graves, Donald E. "'Dry Books of Tactics': U.S. Infantry Manuals of the War of 1812 and After." *Military Historian* 38, no. 2 (1986), 50-61.

_____. "Field Artillery of the War of 1812: Equipment, Organization, Tactics and Effectiveness." *Arms Collecting* 30, no. 2 (1992), 39-48.

_____. "'I have a handsome little army': A Re-examination of Winfield Scott's Camp at Buffalo in 1814." In *War Along the Niagara: Essays on the War of*

1812 and its Legacy, 38-52. R.A. Bowler, ed. Lewiston: Old Fort Niagara Association, 1991.

Green, Ernest. "Township No. 2: Mount Dorchester, Stamford." *Papers and Records of the Ontario Historical Society* 25 (1929), 248-338.

Hofschromb, Peter. "Flintlocks in Battle." *Military Illustrated*, no. 1 (June/July 1986), 29-36.

Kimball, Jeffrey. "The Battle of Chippewa: Infantry Tactics in the War of 1812." *Military Affairs* XXXI, no. 4 (1967-68), 168-186.

Riddell, William R. "The Ancaster 'Bloody Assize' of 1814" *Papers and Records of the Ontario Historical Society* 20 (1923), 108-125.

———. "Joseph Willcocks, Sheriff, Member of Parliament, and Traitor." *Papers and Records of the Ontario Historical Society* 24 (1927), 476-499.

Stagg, John. "Enlisted Men in the United States Army, 1812-1815: A Preliminary Survey." *William and Mary Quarterly*, 3rd Series, 43 (1986), 616-645.

———. "The Politics of Ending the War of 1812." In *War Along the Niagara: Essays on the War of 1812 and Its Legacy*, 93-104. R.A. Bowler, ed. Youngstown, NY: Old Fort Niagara Association, 1991.

Unpublished

Campbell, Brigadier Lorn. "Ideas about Battle, June, 1944." Directorate of History, DND, Ottawa, 171009 (D160).

Couture, Paul. "The Non-Regular Military Forces on the Niagara Frontier: 1812-1814." Ottawa: Canadian Parks Service, Microfiche Report Series, no. 193, 1985.

Graves, Donald E. "The Human Remains of the Battle of Chippawa, 5 July, 1814: A Preliminary Historical Investigation." [Volume I]. Ottawa: unpublished report, Directorate of History, DND, October 1991.

———. "The Human Remains of the Battle of Chippawa, 5 July 1814. Volume II. The Physical Parameters of the Battlefield." Ottawa: unpublished report, Directorate of History, DND, May 1992.

Gray, William. "Soldiers of the Queen: The Militia of Ontario, 1794-1814." Publication forthcoming (September 1994).

Hendry, Douglas. "British Casualties Suffered at Chippawa, 5 July 1814." Ottawa: unpublished research report, Directorate of History, DND, December 1991.

Morris, John. "General Jacob Brown." Siena College, NY: unpublished paper read before the 50th Anniversay Commemorative Conference, 1987.

Schneider, David. "The Training and Organization of General Winfield Scott's Brigade and the Life of the Regular Soldier in it; Niagara Frontier, April - June, 1814." Unpublished M.A. Thesis, University of Florida, 1976.

Index